ANGELA KING'S

S·O·F·T

TOUCHES

ANGELA KING'S

S·O·F·T TOUCHES

STYLISH KNITTING & EMBROIDERY PATTERNS WITH A ROMANTIC LOOK

COLLINS · 8 GRAFTON STREET · LONDON W1X 3LA

First published 1988 by
William Collins Sons & Co. Ltd
London · Glasgow · Sydney
Auckland · Toronto · Johannesburg

British Library Cataloguing in Publication Data
King, Angela
    Soft touches.
    1. Knitting—Patterns
    I. Title
    746.43'2041   TT820

ISBN 0 00 412188 0

Photoset by Ace Filmsetting Ltd, Frome, Somerset
Printed and bound in Spain by Cronion S.A.
Art Director Janet James
Designer Eve White
How-to-knit illustrations by June Tiley
Charts and embroidery illustrations by Judith Rackley
Patterns checked by Janet Bentley

CONTENTS

ACKNOWLEDGEMENTS

PHOTOGRAPHY

Cerise, Aqua, Jade, Turquoise, Twists and Plaits, Argyll Jacket and Sweater, Chenille Cables, Bobbles and Waves, Cornflowers and Wheat, Clove Carnations, Cabbage Roses, Hibiscus, Butterfly, Parma Violet, Crossover, Printout, Birds, Wild Horses, Knife and Fork – MARK LEWIS

For all the above photographs, the Publishers would like to give special thanks to the following:

Models Johnson, Michi, and Jean-Louis
Make-up by Stephanie Jenkins
Hair by Tim Crespin
Stylist – Laura Hardy
Clothes by Helen Storey, Hobbs, Karen Boyd, American Classics, Lunn Antiques
Jewellery from Liberty, Fenwick
Accessories from Liberty, American Classics, Fenwick

Anchor – *Company*, CARRIE BRANOVAN
Hollow Oak and Lorgnette – *Living Magazine*, TONY CHAU
Brilliants, Rhinestones, Lattice – TONY McGEE
Marine, Baby Sailor, Lace, Pearl – MIMA RICHARDSON
Shaggy Dog, Bark, Bone, Knife and Fork – CHRIS CRAYMER
Ribbons – *Woman's Own*, SANDRA LOUSADA

KNITTERS

Many thanks to my loyal and reliable knitters:
   May Begg
   Angela Chapman
   Mandy Goldman
   Marianna Kemmer
   Fusako Maatsura
   Mary Rice
   Harriet Sogbodjor
   Marjorie Vennall

A special sincere thank you to my niece, Sarah Jane Goalen, who did all the embroidery work in this book (except for Parma Violet) and whose patience and care supported me throughout.

Also a special thanks to Brenda Goalen for her technical advice on embroidery and for working the cross stitch for Parma Violet.

INTRODUCTION

Nowadays with so many people leading very busy lives it takes a special reason to justify spending the time knitting. One excellent reason for knitting a garment by hand is to create a garment from a really soft luxurious yarn. In spite of the cost of silk, cashmere or angora, by knitting a garment using these yarns you will have something that would cost at least four times as much in the shops. If you choose a well designed classic shape, the result will more than justify the cost and time spent, since you will enjoy wearing the sweater for many years to come.

Embroidery can add a special touch to a knitted garment, and this book contains some beautifully feminine embroidered designs. Others use appliqué which can be done by quite inexperienced needlewomen. The shapes can be easily cut out as long as you use sharp scissors, and I have only used the five simplest embroidery stitches throughout. If you can embroider but can't knit, the designs would look lovely transferred on to a suitable machine knit. A frill of lace or buttons sewn on as an extra adornment will provide that designer touch and give you the pleasure of wearing something which is uniquely yours.

Certain effects in Aran knitting are still impossible to obtain by machine. Even a simple pattern featuring one huge cable on an easy-to-wear roomy cardigan will be far superior to a machine knit if you choose the right wool, giving that glorious hand-knitted look. And if you can handle complicated Aran patterns, intricate stitches plus beautiful yarn still make an unbeatable combination.

This book is divided into seven very different sections: Silks, using silk yarns in gorgeous glowing colours; Outdoor, containing Aran patterns with traditional stitches such as twists, plaits, bobbles, waves, hartshorn, hollow oak, lorgnette and lattice; Embroidery, with designs decorated with cornflowers, wheat, carnations, cabbage roses, hibiscus, butterflies and parma violets; Delicates, where the designs are in soft feminine colours and yarns; Brights, for day and evening wear; Ethnic Fair Isle, with folk patterns; and Easy Cream, featuring simple but stylish designs which can be knitted up very quickly.

I hope you enjoy knitting the patterns as much as I have enjoyed designing them.

Angela King

KNITTING NOTES

CASTING ON

THE TWO NEEDLE METHOD

Make a slip loop in the yarn, leaving a short length for sewing up. Place the loop on to the left-hand needle. Firmly grasp the short length in the left hand, then inset the point of the right-hand needle behind the loop on the left-hand needle. Wind the yarn round the right-hand needle and draw through. Pass the new loop on to the left-hand needle and tighten.

Insert the right-hand needle between the two loops on the left-hand needle, wind the yarn round the right-hand needle and draw through. Pass the new loop on to the left-hand needle as before.

Continue in this way until you have cast on the required number of stitches.

THE THUMB METHOD
(using only one needle)

Leave a piece of yarn hanging down which is long enough to form the number of stitches required. Make a slip loop and put it on to the needle. Hold the loose end of yarn in your left hand and make a loop on your left thumb. Insert the needle into the loop, wrap the yarn round the needle and draw up through the loop on the thumb as you slip the loop from the thumb and gently tighten the left-hand thread. You have now formed the first stitch. Repeat the process for the rest of the row.

HOW TO KNIT A STITCH

Hold the needle with the cast-on stitches in the left hand. With the yarn at the back of the work, insert the right-hand needle into the front of the first loop on the left-hand needle, front to back, left to right. Wind the yarn round the point of the right-hand needle and draw a loop through the loop on the left-hand needle while slipping this left-hand stitch. The new stitch is now on the right-hand needle.

HOW TO PURL A STITCH

Hold the needle with the cast-on stitches in the left hand. With the yarn at the front of the work, insert the right-hand needle into the front of the first stitch, back to front, right to left.

Take the yarn round the point of the right-hand needle over the top and under, from right to left. Draw this loop through the stitch on the left-hand needle while slipping the left-hand stitch. The new stitch is now on the right-hand needle.

SOME SIMPLE STITCHES

GARTER STITCH
Knit every stitch of every row.

STOCKING STITCH
Knit the first row and purl the second row, repeating these two rows. The knit side is the right side.

REVERSED STOCKING STITCH
Purl the first row, and knit the second row, repeating these two rows. The purl side is the right side.

MOSS STITCH
Knit the first stitch and purl the second stitch, to the end of the row. On the second row, do the opposite: purl all the stitches that face you as knit, and knit all the stitches that face you as purl. Repeat these two rows.

RIBBING
Usually single or double ribbing, although there are others. You work single ribbing by alternating knit and purl stitches to the end of the row. On the second row, you knit all the knit stitches and purl all the purl stitches as they face you.

For double ribbing, work two knit, then two purl stitches to the end of the row, working the stitches as they face you on the second row, and repeat these two rows.

TENSION

If you are following someone else's pattern, you MUST knit to tension. Tension means how tightly or loosely the knitting is worked. If you hate knitting a tension square, do a careful check on the actual work and measure the number of stitches and rows to the number of centimetres or inches quoted at the top of the pattern. If you have fewer stitches than the given tension, change your needles to a size *smaller*. If you have more stitches, change your needles to a size *larger*. Neglect to check this and your garment will probably come out the wrong size.

ABBREVIATIONS

It is vital to read the abbreviations at the beginning of any pattern. These are not standardized and one designer may use the same abbreviation as another, but mean something completely different. So check them before you begin – never assume you know what they mean.

JOINING IN A NEW BALL OF YARN

When starting a new ball of yarn, always join it in at the end of a row – make a knot in the middle of your work and you will get a hole in your sweater. Any long ends will be useful for sewing up afterwards.

MEASUREMENTS

Like checking your tension, measurements must be made with care.

CASTING OFF

Knit the first two stitches of the row. Now lift the second stitch from the point of the right-hand needle over the first stitch, leaving one stitch on this needle. Knit one more stitch and repeat the process. Continue in this way until you only have one stitch left. Cut the yarn and pass it through this stitch, pulling tightly to fasten off.

KNITTING WITH SILK

Knitting with silk is more expensive than knitting with wool, but the rich glowing colours and sensuous feel of the finished product are more than worth the extra money. One consolation is that although the price is roughly three times that of a ball of wool, a ball of silk has greater yardage so will go much further.

Like cotton, silk is inelastic, so you MUST knit firmly. If you are using a wool pattern for your silk, remember that silk does not stretch at all. Loosely worked silk ribbing will drop, so use a smaller needle than you would normally. Knitting with silk is a seductive experience in itself, and unlike wool silk feels wonderful against the skin.

WASHING SILK

Silk is easy to care for, and should be hand-washed avoiding harsh detergents. Use tepid or warm water and do not rub or wring. The use of a fabric conditioner is recommended. Dry the garment by rolling it in a towel first, before laying it out flat to dry thoroughly. Press lightly while still slightly damp, if necessary. A gentle shake will remove any slight stiffness caused by drying.

TRANSFERRING AN EMBROIDERY DESIGN ON TO THE GARMENT

If necessary, enlarge the design from the pattern to the correct size to fit your sweater. The easiest method is to find a photocopying shop with an enlarging service. If you do not live near one, try your local library or adult education centre. One of these is bound to have a machine with an enlarger and you can then check that the enlarged chart fits your garment comfortably.

Then trace the enlarged design on to greaseproof paper, or thin tracing paper. Pin the tracing to the garment. Now tack the outline of the design through the paper, using small stitches. Gently tear the tracing paper away from your tacking.

Blanket stitch

Chain stitch

Small French knot

Simple couching

Long and short satin stitch

ADVICE ON EMBROIDERY

Only the simplest embroidery stitches have been used in this book, and some of the designs can be completed success-fully even if you have never done any embroidery before. French knots, for example, look difficult, but are really very easy to work and they are very effective.

Try to get hold of a proper beading needle for sewing on any sequins or beads. These are very long and fine and will not split your beads.

WORKING APPLIQUÉ

Trace the outline of the appliquéd flower or butterfly on to tracing paper. Pin to shiny fabric (or lace), and wadding, flat-tening slightly with an iron if necessary. Using sharp scissors, cut round the traced outline slightly larger than your tracing. Lightly pencil in all the detail. Tack the tracing to the garment. Neatly blanket stitch the outline in matching thread working french knots, or couching over blanket stitching, as specified by the pattern.

Cross stitch — it is simpler to work one stroke of each cross all along the line then return, crossing each stroke with a second, as long as the crosses are in the same colour

Satin stitch

SILKS

CERISE

**PURE SILK CARDIGAN IN FLAT RIB
WITH CABLED WAIST**

MATERIALS

9(10, 10) 50 g. hanks Filatura di Crosa Silk Top in cerise; a pair each 3¼mm. (no. 10) and 4mm. (no. 8) knitting needles; a 3¼mm. (no. 10) circular needle; a cable needle; 3 buttons.

The quantities of yarn given are based on average requirements and are therefore approximate.

TENSION

30 sts. and 26 rows to 10cm. (4in.) on 4mm. needles over flat rib (not stretched).

MEASUREMENTS

To fit bust: 87(91, 97)cm. (34(36, 38)in.)
Actual measurement (not stretched): 90(94, 98)cm. (35½(37, 38½)in.)
Length from shoulder (inc. bottom band edging): 63(65, 67)cm. (24¾(25½, 26¼)in.)
Sleeve seam: 51(51, 52)cm. (20(20, 20½)in.)

Figures in brackets refer to the larger sizes. Where only one figure is given this refers to all sizes.

ABBREVIATIONS

k. knit; *p.* purl; *st(s).* stitch(es); *WS.* wrong side; *inc.* increase; *alt.* alternate; *dec.* decrease; *C4F.* slip next 4 sts. onto cable needle and hold at front of work, k.4, then k.4 from cable needle; *C4B.* slip next 4 sts. onto cable needle and hold at back of work, k.4, then k.4 from cable needle; *rep.* repeat; *patt.* pattern; *RS.* right side; *foll.* following; *rem.* remaining; *cont.* continue; *beg.* beginning; *cm.* centimetres; *mm.* millimetres; *in.* inches; *g.* grammes.

INSTRUCTIONS

BACK

With 4mm. needles, cast on 132(138, 144) sts. and work in flat rib patt. as follows:

Row 1 (RS): K.5(8, 6), * p.2, k.8, rep. from * to last 7(10, 8) sts., p.2, k.5(8, 6).

Row 2: P.5(8, 6), * k.2, p.8, rep. from * to last 7(10, 8) sts., k.2, p.5(8, 6).

These 2 rows form the flat rib patt.

Rep. these 2 rows 23(24, 25) times in all – 46(48, 50) rows.

CABLE FOR WAIST SHAPING

Next row (RS): K.5(8, 6), * p.2, C4F., rep. from * to last 7(10, 8) sts., p.2, k.5(8, 6).

Next row: As row 2 of flat rib patt. Rep. the 2 rows of flat rib 3 times, then work the 2 cable rows again. Cont. in this way until you have worked the 2 cable rows 4 times in all.

Now cont. straight in flat rib for a further 86(90, 94) rows, ending with a WS row.

SHAPE SHOULDERS

Keeping flat rib correct, cast off 20 sts. at beg. of next 2 rows and 22(23, 24) sts. at beg. of foll. 2 rows. Cast off rem. 48(52, 56) sts.

RIGHT FRONT

With 4mm. needles, cast on 35(38, 41) sts., and shape front as follows:

Row 1 (RS): Inc. into first st., k.7(7, 2), * p.2, k.8, rep. from * to last 7(10, 8) sts., p.2, k.5(8, 6).

Row 2: P.5(8, 6), * k.2, p.8, rep. from * to last 1(1, 6) st(s)., k.1(1, 2), p.0(0, 4).

Cont. to rep. these 2 rows, but inc. 1 st. at same edge (front edge) on every row to 56(59, 62) sts., working inc. sts. into patt. Now inc. 1 st. at same edge on every alt. row to 66(69, 72) sts.

Work 4(6, 8) rows straight in patt. thus ending with a WS row.

CABLE FOR WAIST SHAPING

Next row: K.9(9, 4), * p.2, C4F., rep. from * to last 7(10, 8) sts., p.2, k.5(8, 6).

When you have cabled 4 times in all, as for back, work straight in flat rib patt. for a further 16(14, 12) rows.

SHAPE NECK

Keeping flat rib correct, dec. 1 st. at neck edge on next row and then at this edge on every foll. 3rd row to 42(43, 44) sts.

Work 1 row straight, thus ending at side edge. (Front measures the same as back to beg. of shoulder shaping.)

SHAPE SHOULDER

Keeping flat rib correct, cast off 20 sts. at beg. of next row.

Work 1 row. Cast off rem. 22(23, 24) sts.

LEFT FRONT

Work as for Right Front, but reversing all shapings and flat rib patt., and reversing cable patt. by working C4B. instead of C4F.

SLEEVES
(make 2)

With 3¼mm. needles, cast on 48(48, 54) sts. and work in k.1, p.1, rib for 17 rows, working 20 incs. evenly spaced along last row – 68(68, 74) sts.

Change to 4mm. needles, and work in flat rib patt. as follows:

Row 1 (RS): K.8(8, 6), * p.2, k.8, rep. from * to last 10(10, 8) sts., p.2, k.8(8, 6).

Row 2: P.8(8, 6), * k.2, p.8, rep. from * to last 10(10, 8) sts., k.2, p.8(8, 6).

Rep. these 2 rows until 16 rows in all have been worked.

Now inc. 1 st. at each end of next row and then every foll. 4th row until there are 112(112, 118) sts. on the needle, working inc. sts. into patt. Now cont. straight until sleeve measures 51(51, 52)cm. (20(20, 20½)in.) from cast-on edge, ending with a WS row.

Cast off.

MAKING UP

Join shoulder seams. With centre of cast-off edges of sleeves to shoulder seams, sew sleeves carefully in position, reaching down to same depth on front and back. Join side and sleeve seams.

EDGING
(worked in sections)

With the 3¼mm. circular needle and RS facing and starting at right shoulder edge, pick up and k.48 sts. along back neck edge, 62(64, 66) sts. down left front sloping edge, 44 sts. along straight front edge and finally 44 sts. along curved edge of left front, ending where curve ends – 198(200, 202) sts.

Work backwards and forwards in rows and work in k.1, p.1, rib for 9 rows. Cast off in rib.

With 3¼mm. needles and RS facing, pick up and k.112(116, 120) sts. along bottom straight edge of garment. Work 9 rows in k.1, p.1, rib. Cast off in rib.

With 3¼mm. needles and RS facing and beg. at bottom curved edge of right front, pick up and k.44 sts. along curved edge, 44 sts. along straight front edge, and finally 62(64, 66) sts. up right front sloping edge – 150(152, 154) sts.

Work in k.1, p.1, rib for 3 rows.

Buttonhole row (RS): Rib 46, cast off 2 sts., * rib 16, cast off 2 sts., rep. from * once more, rib to end.

Next row: Rib to end, but cast on 2 sts. 3 times in place of those cast off on previous row. When the 9th rib row has been completed, cast off in rib. Join band on the wrong side at bottom edges and at right shoulder. Sew on buttons to correspond with buttonholes.

If you like an even more fitted waist, take the seams in at the sides of the cabling.

JADE AQUA

JADE

SILK FITTED TUNIC WITH LONG SLEEVES AND ROUND NECKLINE

MATERIALS

9(10, 11) 50 g. hanks Rowan Mulberry Silk in jade; a pair each 2¾mm. (no. 12) and 3mm. (no. 11) knitting needles; spare needle.

The quantities of yarn given are based on average requirements and are therefore approximate.

TENSION

28 sts. and 37 rows to 10cm. (4in.) on 3mm. needles over st.st.

MEASUREMENTS

To fit bust: 87(91, 97)cm. (34(36, 38)in.)
Actual measurement: 100(106, 112)cm. (39¼(41¾, 44)in.)
Lenghth from shoulder: 60(61, 62)cm. (23½(24, 24½)in.)
Sleeve seam: 49cm. (19¼in.)
Figures in brackets refer to the larger sizes. Where only one figure is given this refers to all sizes.

ABBREVIATIONS

k. knit; *p.* purl; *st(s).* stitch(es); *inc.* increase; *dec.* decrease; *st.st.* stocking stitch; *alt.* alternate; *beg.* beginning; *tog.* together; *M1* pick up horizontal loop lying between st. just worked and following st. and work into the back of it; *rem.* remaining; *cont.* continue; *rep.* repeat; *foll.* following; *RS.* right side; *WS.* wrong side; *mm.* millimetres; *g.* grammes; *cm.* centimetres; *in.* inches; *dec. 2* slip one st., knit 2 sts. together, pass slipped st. over.

BACK

With 2¾mm. needles, cast on 121(129, 137)sts. by the thumb method, and work in single rib as follows:
Row 1: K.1, * p.1, k.1, rep. from * to end.
Row 2: P.1, * k.1, p.1, rep. from * to end.
Rep. last 2 rows until 23 rib rows have been worked in all, working 20 incs evenly spaced along last row – 141(149, 157)sts.
Change to 3mm. needles, and starting with a k. row, work in st.st. for 20 rows.

WORK SHAPINGS

Next row: K.34(36, 38), dec. 2, k.67(71, 75), dec. 2, k.34(36, 38).
Starting with a p. row, work in st.st. for 3 rows.
Next row: K.33(35, 37), dec. 2, k.65(69, 73), dec. 2, k.33(35, 37).

Starting with a p. row work in st.st. for 3 rows.
Cont. in this way, dec. on next row and then on every foll. 4th row, working 1 st. less at beg. and end of each dec. row and 2 sts. less at centre until 105(113, 121) sts. remain, ending with a dec. row.
Starting with a p. row work in st.st. for a further 19 rows.
* *Next row (RS):* K.27(29, 31), M1, k. to last 27(29, 31) sts., M1, k. to end.
Starting with a p. row work in st.st. for 3 rows. *
Rep. from * to * until there are 141(149, 157) sts. on the needle, ending with 1 p. row, instead of 3 st.st. rows.

SHAPE ARMHOLES

Cast off 8 sts. at beg. of next 2 rows. Now dec. 1 st. at each end of every foll. alt. row until 101(109, 117) sts. remain.
Now cont. straight until armholes measure 20(21, 22)cm (8(8¼, 8¾)in.) from beg. of shaping, ending with a RS row.

SHAPE SHOULDERS AND BACK NECK

Next row: P.29(33, 37), cast off centre 43 sts., p. to end of row and cont. on this last set of sts. only.
** Cast off 12(14, 16) sts. at beg. (armhole edge) of next row and 13(15, 17) sts. at beg. of foll. alt. row, *at the same time*, dec. 1 st. at neck edge on the next 4 rows. Fasten off.
With RS facing rejoin yarn to rem. sts. and k. to end of row. Now work as for first side from ** to end.

FRONT

Work as for back until armholes measure 13(14, 15)cm. (5(5½, 6)in.) from beg. of shaping, ending with a RS row.

SHAPE FRONT NECK

Next row: K.38(42, 46), k.2 tog., turn, and work on this first set of sts. only.
*** Dec. 1 st. at neck edge on every row until 25(29, 33) sts. remain.
Now cont. straight until front measures same as back to beg. of shoulder shaping, ending at armhole edge.

SHAPE SHOULDER

Cast off 12(14, 16) sts. at beg. of next row. Work 1 row. Cast off rem. 13(15, 17) sts.

A Q U A

PURE SILK CROPPED CARDIGAN
IN STOCKING STITCH

Return to rem. sts. and slip centre 21 sts. onto a spare needle, with RS facing rejoin yarn to rem sts., k.2 tog., and k. to end of row.

Now work as for first side from *** to end.

SLEEVES
(make 2)

With 2¾mm. needles, cast on 67(71, 75) sts. by the thumb method, and work in single rib as for back welt for 7cm. (2¾in.), working 17 incs. evenly spaced across last row – 84(88, 92) sts.

Change to 3mm. needles, and starting with a k. row, work in st.st., inc. 1 st. at each end of every foll. 8th row until 110(114, 118) sts. are on the needle.

Now cont. straight until sleeve measures 49cm. (19¼in.) from cast-on edge, ending with a WS row.

SHAPE TOP

Cast off 8 sts. at beg. of next 2 rows – 94(98, 102) sts.

Now dec. 1 st. at each end of every foll. alt. row until 60(64, 68) sts. remain, then at each end of every row until 24 sts. remain.

Cast off 3 sts. at beg. of next 2 rows, then cast off rem. 18 sts.

NECKBAND

Join right shoulder seam.

With 2¾mm. needles, and RS facing, pick up and k. 36 sts. down left front neck, k. across centre 21 sts. of front, pick up and k. 36 sts. up right front neck, and 62 sts. across back neck – 155 sts.

Starting with a 2nd row, work in single rib as for back welt for 9 rows.

Cast off ribwise.

MAKING UP

Join left shoulder and neckband seam. Sew sleeves into armholes easing to fit. Join side and sleeve seams. Press all seams.

MATERIALS

6(7, 7) 50 g. hanks Filatura di Crosa Silk Top in pale blue; a pair each 3¾mm. (no. 9) and 4mm. (no. 8) knitting needles; 3 buttons.

The quantities of yarn given are based on average requirements and are therefore approximate.

TENSION

24 sts. and 26 rows to 10cm. (4in.) on 4mm. needles over st.st.

MEASUREMENTS

To fit bust: 87(91, 97)cm. (34(36, 38)in.)
Actual measurement: 114(118, 121)cm. (45(46½, 47¾)in.)
Length from shoulder: 40(41, 42)cm. (15¾(16, 16½)in.)
Sleeve seam: approx. 46cm. (18in.)
Figures in brackets refer to the larger sizes. Where only one figure is given this refers to all sizes.

ABBREVIATIONS

k. knit; *p.* purl; *st(s).* stitch(es); *inc.* increase; *rep.* repeat; *foll.* following; *rem.* remaining; *st.st.* stocking stitch; *beg.* beginning; *approx.* approximately; *cm.* centimetres; *mm.* millimetres; *in.* inches; *RS.* right side; *WS.* wrong side; *tog.* together; *dec.* decrease; *cont.* continue; *g.* grammes.

INSTRUCTIONS

BACK

With 3¾mm. needles, cast on 135(139, 143) sts., and work in single rib as follows:
Row 1 (RS): K.1, * p.1, k.1, rep. from * to end.
Row 2: P.1, * k.1, p.1, rep. from * to end.
Rep. last 2 rows until 12 rib rows have been worked in all, working an inc. at each end of last row ** – 137(141, 145) sts.
Change to 4mm. needles, and starting with a k. row work in st.st. until back measures 38(39, 40)cm. (15(15¼, 15¾)in.) from cast-on edge, ending with a WS row.

SHAPE BACK NECK

Next row: K.48(50, 52), k.2 tog., turn, and work on these sts. only. *** Dec. 1 st. at neck edge on every row until 46(48, 50) sts. remain ending at side edge.

SHAPE SHOULDER

Cast off 24 sts. at beg. of next row.
Dec. 1 st. at neck edge at beg. of foll. row.
Cast off rem. 21(23, 25) sts.
With RS facing return to rem. sts., cast off centre 37 sts., k.2 tog., k. to end of row.
Work 1 row.
Now work as for first side from *** to end.

RIGHT FRONT

With 3¾mm. needles, cast on 65(67, 69) sts., and work as for back welt to ** – 67(69, 71)sts.
Change to 4mm. needles and starting with a k. row work in st.st. until front measures 16(17, 18)cm (6¼(6¾, 7)in.) from cast-on edge, ending with a WS row.

SHAPE FRONT NECK

Dec. 1 st. at neck edge on next row and at this edge on every foll. 3rd row until 46(48, 50) sts. remain.
Work a few rows straight until front measures same as back to beg. of shoulder shaping, ending at side edge.

SHAPE SHOULDER

Cast off 24 sts. at beg. of next row.
Dec. 1 st. at neck edge at beg. of foll. row.
Cast off rem. 21(23, 25) sts.

LEFT FRONT

Work as for Right Front, but reversing all shapings.

SLEEVES
(make 2)

With 3¾mm. needles, cast on 43(47, 51) sts., and work in single rib as for back welt for 7 cm. (2¾in.) ending with a 2nd row and working 17 incs. evenly spaced along last row – 60(64, 68) sts.
Change to 4mm. needles and starting with a k. row work in st.st., but inc. 1 st. at each end of every foll. 4th row until there are 110(114, 118) sts. on the needle.
Work 2 rows straight, then cast off.

MAKING UP

Join shoulder seams. With centre of cast-off edges of sleeves to shoulder seams, sew sleeves carefully in position, reaching down to same depth on front and back. Join side and sleeve seams.

FRONT BAND

With 3¾mm. needles, cast on 12 sts. and work in k.1, p.1, rib for 4 rows.
** *Buttonhole row (RS):* Rib 5, cast off 2 sts., rib 5.
Next row: Rib 5, cast on 2 sts., rib 5.
Rib 18 more rows.
Cont. to rep. from ** until the third buttonhole has been completed. Now cont. straight in rib until band, when slightly stretched, fits around front and back neck edges, sewing in position as you go along. Cast off ribwise.
Sew on buttons to correspond with buttonholes.

TURQUOISE

FITTED SILK CARDIGAN WITH SNAKY CABLES

MATERIALS

5(6, 6) 50 g. hanks Filatura di Crosa Silk Top in turquoise; a pair each 3¼mm. (no. 10) and 4mm. (no. 8) knitting needles; a cable needle; 3 buttons.

The quantities of yarn given are based on average requirements and are therefore approximate.

TENSION

24 sts. and 26 rows to 10cm. (4in.) on 4mm. needles over st.st.

MEASUREMENTS

To fit bust: 87(91, 97)cm. (34(36, 38)in.)
Actual measurement: 96(101, 106)cm. (37¾(39¾, 41¾)in.)
Length from shoulder: 43(44, 45)cm. (17(17¼, 17¾)in.)
Sleeve seam: 16cm. (6¼in.)
Figures in brackets refer to the larger sizes. Where only one figure is given this refers to all sizes.

ABBREVIATIONS

k. knit; *p.* purl; *st(s).* stitch(es); *inc.* increase; *alt.* alternate; *dec.* decrease; *C3F.* slip next 3 sts. onto cable needle and hold at front of work, k.3, then k.3 from cable needle; *C3B.* slip next 3 sts. onto cable needle and hold at back of work, k.3, then k.3 from cable needle; *patt.* pattern; *foll.* following; *RS.* right side; *WS.* wrong side; *cm.* centimetres; *mm.* millimetres; *in.* inches; *rep.* repeat; *cont.* continue; *beg.* beginning; *rem.* remaining; *st.st.* stocking stitch; *g.* grammes.

BACK

With 3¼mm. needles, cast on 110(114, 118) sts. and work in double rib as follows:

Row 1 (RS): K.2, * p.2, k.2, rep. from * to end.

Row 2: P.2, * k.2, p.2, rep. from * to end.

Rep. last 2 rows until rib measures 9cm. (3½in.), ending with a 2nd row and working 10 incs. evenly spaced along last row – 120(124, 128) sts.

Change to 4mm. needles, and work in patt. as follows:

Row 1 (RS): P.3(5, 1), * k.6, p.6, rep. from * to last 9(11, 7) sts., k.6, p.3(5, 1).

Row 2: K.3(5, 1), * p.6, k.6, rep. from * to last 9(11, 7) sts., p.6, k.3(5, 1).

Rep. last 2 rows twice more.

Row 7: P.3(5, 1), * C3F., p.6, rep. from * to last 9(11, 7) sts., C3F., p.3(5, 1).

Row 8: As row 2.

Rep. rows 1 and 2 three times more.

Row 15: P.3(5, 1), * C3B., p.6, rep. from * to last 9(11, 7) sts., C3B., p.3(5, 1).

Row 16: As row 2.

These 16 rows from the pattern and are repeated throughout.

Cont. straight in patt. until back measures 18(19, 20)cm. (7(7½, 8)in.) from cast-on edge, ending with a WS row.

SHAPE ARMHOLES

Keeping patt. correct, cast off 5 sts. at beg. of next 2 rows.

Dec. 1 st. at each end of the foll. alt. row, then on the 6th foll. row, and then the foll. 12th row – 104(108, 112) sts.

Now cont. straight in patt. until back measures 40(41, 42)cm. (15¾(16, 16½)in.) from cast-on edge, ending with a WS row.

SHAPE BACK NECK

Next row: patt. 39(41, 43), cast off centre 26 sts., patt. to end of row, and work on this last set of sts only.

Work 1 row.

** Cast off 4 sts. at beg. (neck edge) on next row, 3 sts. at beg. of foll. alt. row and 2 sts. on next alt. row.

Work 1 row, thus ending with a WS row.

Cast off rem. 30(32, 34) sts.

With WS facing rejoin yarn to rem. sts. and work as for first side from ** to end, but work 2 rows straight before shoulder cast-off.

LEFT FRONT

With 3¼mm. needles, cast on 52(56, 60) sts., and work in k.2, p.2 rib for 9cm. (3½in.), ending with a WS row and working 8 incs. evenly spaced along last row – 60(64, 68) sts.

Change to 4mm. needles, and work in patt. as for back until front measures 14(15, 15)cm. (5½(6, 6)in.) from cast-on edge, ending with a WS row.

SHAPE FRONT NECK

Keeping patt. correct, dec. 1 st. at neck edge on next row and then at this edge on every foll. 3rd row, *at the same time*, when front measures 18(19, 20)cm. (7(7½, 8)in.) from cast-on edge, ending at side edge, cont. as follows:

SHAPE ARMHOLE

Keeping patt. correct, and neck decs. correct, cast off 5 sts. at beg. of next row, and then dec. 1 st. at same edge on the foll. alt. row, then 1 st. on the foll. 6th row and foll. 12th row.

Now keeping armhole edge straight, cont. to dec. at neck edge as set on every foll. 3rd row until 30(32, 34) sts. remain.

Now work straight until front measures the same as back to cast-off shoulder edge, ending with a WS row.

Cast off all sts.

RIGHT FRONT

Work as for Left Front, but reversing all shapings and reversing cable patt. by working C3B. on row 7 and C3F. on row 15.

SLEEVES

(make 2)

(*NB.* Reverse cable patt. for second sleeve as for fronts.)

With 3¼mm. needles, cast on 70(70, 74) sts., and work in double rib as for back welt for 7cm. (2¾in.) ending with a 2nd row and working 14 incs. evenly spaced along last row – 84(84, 88) sts.

Change to 4mm. needles, and work in patt. as follows:

Row 1 (RS): P.3(3, 5), * k.6, p.6, rep. from * to last 9(9, 11) sts., k.6, p.3(3, 5).

The patt. is now placed. Cont. to work in patt. as for back until 22 patt. rows in all have been worked, thus ending with a WS row.

SHAPE TOP

Keeping patt. correct, cast off 8 sts. at beg. of next 2 rows.

Now dec. 1 st. at each end of every foll. alt. row until 40(40, 44) sts. remain.

Now cast off 3 sts. at beg. of next 6 rows, then cast off rem. 22(22, 26) sts.

MAKING UP

Join shoulder seams. With centre of cast-off edges of sleeves to shoulder seams, carefully sew sleeves into armholes. Join side and sleeve seams.

FRONT BAND

With 3¼mm. needles cast on 12 sts., and work in k.2, p.2, rib for 4 rows.

** *Buttonhole row (RS):* Rib 5, cast off 2 sts., rib. 5.

Next row: Rib 5, cast on 2 sts, rib 5.

Rib 20 more rows.

Cont. to rep. from ** until the third buttonhole has been completed.

Now cont. straight in rib until band, when slightly stretched, fits around front and back neck edges, sewing in position as you go along.

Cast off ribwise.

Sew on buttons to correspond with buttonholes.

MARINE

CHILD'S STRIPED SILK T-SHIRT, WITH CABLED WELT AND NECKBAND

MATERIALS

2 50 g. hanks Filatura di Crosa Silk Top in each of the following colours: grey, navy, black and white.

or 2 50g. balls Pingouin Coton Naturel 8 Fils in each of the following colours: grey, navy, black and white.

A pair each 3¾mm. (no. 9) and 4mm. (no. 8) knitting needles; 2 spare needles.

The quantities of yarn given are based on average requirements and are therefore approximate.

TENSION

24 sts. and 26 rows to 10cm. (4in.) on 4mm. needles over st.st.

MEASUREMENTS

To fit chest: 67(71)cm. (26(28)in.)

Actual measurement: 75(80)cm. (29½(31½)in.)

Length from shoulder: 44(45)cm. (17¼(17¾)in.)

Sleeve seam: 2.5(3)cm. (1(1¼)in.).

Figures in brackets refer to the larger size. Where only one figure is given this refers to both sizes.

ABBREVIATIONS

k. knit; *p.* purl; *st(s).* stitch(es); *inc.* increase; *dec.* decrease; *st.st.* stocking stitch; *beg.* beginning; *tog.* together; *Tr2* k. into the 2nd st., on left-hand needle, then into the first, slipping both sts. off the needle together; *cm.* centimetres; *mm.* millimetres; *in.* inches; *g.* grammes; *RS.* right side; *WS.* wrong side; *rep.* repeat; *cont.* continue; *rem.* remaining.

BACK & FRONT
(both alike)

With 3¾mm. needles and grey, cast on 88(93) sts. and work in cabled rib as follows:

Row 1 (RS): * P.3, Tr2, rep. from * to last 3 sts., p.3.

Row 2: * K.3, p.2, rep. from * to last 3 sts., k.3.

Rep. these 2 rows 9 times in all, working 2(3) incs. evenly spaced across last row – 90(96) sts.

Change to 4mm. needles, and starting with a k. row work in st.st. until grey measures 11cm. (4¼in.) from cast-on edge, ending with a WS row.

Change to black and cont. in st.st. for a further 11cm. (4¼in.) ending with a WS row.

Change to white and cont. in st.st. for a further 5cm. (2in.) ending with a WS row.

SHAPE SLEEVES

Cast on 6(8) sts. at beg. of next 2 rows – 102(112) sts.

Cont. in white until this stripe measures 11cm. (4¼in.) ending with a WS row.

Change to navy and work in st.st. for a further 5cm. (2in.) ending with a WS row.

SHAPE NECK

Next row: K.30(35), k.2 tog., turn, and work on this first set of sts. only.

** Dec. 1 st. at neck edge on next 5(6) rows – 26(30) sts.

Work 4(7) rows straight, thus ending with a WS row.

Cast off.

Return to rem. sts. and slip centre 38 sts. onto a spare needle. With RS facing rejoin navy to rem. sts. K.2 tog., and k. to end of row.

Now work as for first side from ** to end.

NECKBAND

Join right shoulder seam.

With 3¾mm. needles and navy and RS facing, pick up and k. 13(14) sts. down left front neck, k. across the 38 sts. at centre front, pick up and k. 12(13) sts. up right front neck, 12(13) sts. down right back neck, k. across the 38 sts. at centre back, then pick up and k. 13(15) sts. up left back neck – 126(131) sts.

Now work in cabled rib as follows:

Row 1 (WS): K.2, * p.2, k.3, rep. from * to last 4 sts., p.2, k.2.

Row 2: P.2, * Tr2., p.3, rep. from * to last 4 sts., Tr2., p.2.

Rep. last 2 rows 3 times in all.

Cast off in rib patt.

MAKING UP

Join left shoulder seam and neckband. Join side seams and sleeve seams.

OUTDOOR

TWISTS & PLAITS

CARDIGAN COAT WITH MEDALLION AND UPWARDS AND DOWNWARDS PLAIT CABLES

MATERIALS

29 50 g. balls Emu Supermatch Chunky in cream; a pair each 4½mm. (no. 7) and 5½mm. (no. 5) knitting needles; a cable needle; 8 large buttons; spare needles; 2 safety pins.

The quantities of yarn given are based on average requirements and are therefore approximate.

TENSION

16 sts. and 22 rows to 10cm. (4in.) on 5½mm. needles over st.st.

MEASUREMENTS

To fit bust: 87–101cm. (34–40in.) – one size only.
Actual measurement: 138cm. (54½in.)
Length from shoulder: 106cm. (41¾in.)
Sleeve seam: 51cm. (20in.)

ABBREVIATIONS

k. knit; *p.* purl; *st(s).* stitch(es); *inc.* increase; *foll.* following; *patt.* pattern; *C3F.* slip next 3 sts. onto cable needle and hold at front of work, k.3 then k.3 from cable needle; *C3B.* slip next 3 sts. onto cable needle and hold at back of work, k.3 then k.3 from cable needle; *RS.* right side; *WS.* wrong side; *C5F.* slip next 5 sts. onto cable needle and hold at front of work, k.5, then k.5 from cable needle; *C5B.* slip next 5 sts. onto cable needle and hold at back of work, k.5 then k.5 from cable needle; *C4F.* slip next 4 sts. onto cable needle and hold at front of work, k.4 then k.4 from cable needle; *C4B.* slip next 4 sts. onto cable needle and hold at back of work, k.4 then k.4 from cable needle; *T2r.* pass the right-hand needle in front of the first st. on left-hand needle, k. into the front of the next st. on the left-hand needle then k. into the front of the first missed st., and slip both sts. off the needle together; *st.st.* stocking stitch; *cm.* centimetres; *mm.* millimetres; *in.* inches; *g.* grammes; *rep.* repeat; *cont.* continue; *beg.* beginning; *tog.* together; *rem.* remaining; *dec.* decrease.

PATT. A

10 stitch cable (cabled forward)

Row 1 (RS): K.
Row 2 and alt. rows: P.
Rep. these 2 rows twice more.
Row 7: C5B.
Row 8: As row 2.
Rep. rows 1 and 2 twice more.
These 12 rows form *Patt. A* and are repeated as required.

PATT. B

Medallion Cable (worked over 13 sts.)

Row 1 (RS): K.
Row 2 and alt. rows: P.
Rep. these 2 rows once more.
Row 5: C3F., k.1, C3B.
Row 7: As row 1.
Rep. the last 2 rows twice more.
Row 13: C3B., k.1, C3F.
Row 15: As row 1.
Row 16: As row 2.
These 16 rows form *Patt. B* and are repeated as required.

PATT. C

Upwards Plait (worked over 12 sts.)

Row 1 (RS): K.
Row 2 and alt. rows: P.
Row 3: C4B., k.4.
Rows 5 and 7: K.
Row 9: K.4, C4F.
Row 11: K.
Row 12: P.
These 12 rows form *Patt. C* and are repeated as required.

PATT. D

Downwards Plait (worked over 12 sts.)

Row 1 (RS): K.
Row 2 and alt. rows: P.
Row 3: C4F., k.4.
Rows 5 and 7: K.
Row 9: K.4, C4B.
Row 11: K.
Row 12: P.
These 12 rows form *Patt. D* and are repeated as required.

PATT. E

10 stitch cable (cabled backwards)

As Patt. A, but on row 7, C5F.

BACK

With 4½mm. needles, cast on 126 sts., and work in double rib as follows:
Row 1 (RS): K.2, * p.2, k.2, rep. from * to end.
Row 2: P.2, * k.2, p.2, rep. from * to end.
Rep. last 2 rows until rib measures 8cm. (3in.), ending with a 2nd row and working 28 incs. evenly spaced along last row – 154 sts.
Change to 5½mm. needles, and place patterns as follows:
Row 1 (RS): P.2, work over the next 10 sts. as row 1 of *Patt. A*, p.1, T2r., p.1, work over the next 13 sts. as row 1 of *Patt. B*, p.1, T2r., p.1, work over the next 12 sts. as row 1 of *Patt. C*, p.2, work over the next 12 sts. as row 1 of *Patt. D*, p.1, T2r., p.1, work over the next 13 sts. as row 1 of *Patt. B*, p.2, work over the next 13 sts. as row 1 of *Patt. B*, p.1, T2r., p.1, work over the next 12 sts. as row 1 of *Patt. D*, p.2, work over the next 12 sts. as row 1 of *Patt. C*, p.1, T2r., p.1, work over the next 13 sts. as row 1 of *Patt. B*, p.1, T2r., p.1, work over the next 10 sts. as row 1 of *Patt. E*, p.2.
This sets the foundation row of all the patterns. Cont. to rep. the various pattern rows as required until 216 rows of patt. have been worked in all, thus ending with a WS row. (Patts. A, C, D and E have been repeated 18 times in all.)

SHAPE SHOULDERS

Keeping patts. correct, cast off 25 sts. at beg. of next 2 rows, then cast off 24 sts. at beg. of foll. 2 rows, working k.2 tog. across each cable as you cast off.
Over the rem. 56 sts., work 22 decs., then leave the rem. 34 sts. for back neck on a spare needle.

RIGHT FRONT

With 4½mm. needles, cast on 62 sts. and work in double rib as for back welt for 8cm. (3in.), ending with a 2nd row and working 16 incs. evenly spaced along last row – 78 sts.
Change to 5½mm. needles, and place patterns as follows:
Row 1 (RS): P.2, work over the next 13 sts. as row 1 of *Patt. B*, p.1, T2r., p.1, work over the next 12 sts. as row 1 of *Patt. D.*, p.2, work over the next 12 sts. as row 1 of *Patt. C*, p.1, T2r., p.1, work over the next 13 sts. as row 1 of *Patt. B*, p.1, T2r., p.1,

work over the next 10 sts. as row 1 of *Patt. A*, p.2.
This sets the foundation row of all the patterns. Cont. to rep. the various pattern rows as required until 90 rows of patt. have been worked in all, thus ending with a WS row. Leave these sts. on a spare needle.

POCKET LININGS
(make 2)

With 5½mm. needles, cast on 24 sts., and starting with a k. row work in st.st. for 23 rows, working 4 incs. evenly spaced over last row – 28 sts., and ending with a RS row.
Leave sts. on a spare needle.

PLACE POCKETS

Return to right front sts., and keeping patts. correct. cont. as follows:
Next row (RS): Patt. to last 32 sts., cast off the next 16 sts. (working k.2 tog. 6 times over *Patt. B* as you cast off), patt. to end of row.
Next row: Patt. 16 sts., then cont. in patt. over the 28 sts. of first pocket lining, turn, and cont. in patt. over these 44 sts. ONLY until 12 patt. rows have been completed. Return to the rem. 46 sts. of row, patt. to match, but dec. 1 st. at inside (pocket) edge on every row until 34 sts. remain.
Now working over all the 78 sts., cont. in patts. as set until 208 patt. rows have been worked in all, thus ending with a WS row.

SHAPE FRONT NECK

Keeping patts. correct, cast off 24 sts. at beg. (neck edge) of next row (working 10 decs. as you go), patt. to end.
Now dec. 1 st. at neck edge on every row until 49 sts. remain.
Now cont. straight in patts. until front measures the same as back to beg. of shoulder shaping, ending at side edge.

SHAPE SHOULDER

Keeping patts. correct, cast off 25 sts. (working decs. over cables as you cast off), patt. to end.
Work 1 row.
Cast off rem. 24 sts., working decs. over cables as before.

LEFT FRONT

Work as for right front but reverse position of patterns as follows:
Row 1 (RS): P.2, work over the next 10 sts. as row 1 of *Patt. E*, p.1, T2r., p.1, work over the next 13 sts. as row 1 of *Patt. B*, p.1, T2r., p.1, work over the next 12 sts. as row 1 of *Patt. C*, p.2, work over the next 12 sts. as row 1 of *Patt. D*, p.1, T2r., p.1, work over the next 13 sts. as row 1 of *Patt. B*, p.2.
Cont. as for right front and work pocket opening as follows:
Next row (RS): Patt. 16, put these sts. on a spare needle, cast off the next 16 sts. (working 6 decs. over cable) patt. to end of row.
Cont. to work in patts. over last set of sts. only, but dec. 1 st. at pocket edge on every row until 34 sts. remain. Leave sts. on a spare needle. Now patt. across the 28 sts. of 2nd pocket lining, patt. 16 sts. from spare needle.
Complete as for right front.

SLEEVES
(make 2 – worked from top edge downwards)

With 5½mm. needles, cast on 116 sts., and place patterns as for back as follows:
Row 1 (RS): (P.2, k.10) twice, p.1, T2r., p.1, k.13, p.1, T2r., p.1, k.12, p.2, k.12, p.1, T2r., p.1, k.13, p.1, T2r., p.1, (k.10, p.2) twice.
The k. sts. are worked over patts. in the following order:
Patts. A, A, B, D, C, B, E, E.
Patt. 8 rows straight.
Now dec. 1 st. at each end of next row and then every foll. 4th row until 72 sts. remain.
Work a few rows straight in patts. until 96 patt. rows in all have been worked, working 30 decs. evenly spaced over last row – 42 sts.
Change to 4½mm. needles, and work in double rib as for back welt for 8cm. (3in.). Cast off fairly loosely ribwise.

FRONT BANDS

Join shoulder seams.
With 4½mm. needles, cast on 16 sts., and work in k.2, p.2, rib for 14 rows.
*** Buttonhole row (RS):* Rib 7, cast off 2 sts., rib 7.

Next row: Rib 7, cast on 2 sts., rib 7.
Rib 28 more rows.
Cont. to rep. from ** until the 7th button-hole has been completed, and 24 rib rows have been worked. Leave sts. on a safety pin.
Work another band to match, but omit the buttonholes.

NECKBAND

With 4½mm. needles and RS facing, rib across the 16 sts. of buttonhole band, pick up and k. 29 sts. up right front neck edge, work in k.2, p.2, rib over the 34 sts. of back neck, pick up and k. 29 sts. down left front neck and finally rib across the 16 sts. of button band – 124 sts.
Keeping rib patt. correct, rib 3 rows.
Buttonhole row (RS): Rib 7, cast off 2 sts, rib to end.
Next row: Rib to last 7 sts., cast on 2 sts., rib to end.
Work 10 more rows in rib, then rep. the 2 buttonhole rows once more.
Rib 4 rows, then cast off fairly loosely ribwise.

MAKING UP

With centre of cast-on edges of sleeves to shoulder seams, sew sleeves carefully in position, stretching top of sleeve slightly to give an armhole depth of 28cm. (11in.) on front and back.
Join side and sleeve seams. Fold neck-band in half to inside and carefully stitch in position, stitching around buttonhole. Stitch on front bands stretching slightly to fit. Sew on buttons to correspond with buttonholes. Sew down pocket linings.

POCKET EDGINGS
(alike)

With 4½mm. needles and RS facing, pick up and k. 34 sts. along curved edge of one pocket. Starting with a 2nd row, work in double rib as for back welt for 7 rows.
Cast off fairly loosely ribwise.
Catch stitch sides of edgings in position.
Press all seams.

JACKET   ARGYLL SWEATER

ARGYLL JACKET

ARGYLL CARDIGAN WITH POCKETS SET INTO THE SEAMS

MATERIALS

15(16, 17) 50 g. balls Sirdar Country Style Chunky in cream; 2(2, 3) balls in black; 1(1, 1) ball in grey; a pair each 5½mm. (no. 5) and 6mm. (no. 4) knitting needles; 5 toggles (or buttons).

The quantities of yarn given are based on average requirements and are therefore approximate.

TENSION

15 sts. and 20 rows to 10cm. (4in.) on 6mm. needles over st.st.

MEASUREMENTS

To fit bust: 87(91, 97)cm. (34(36, 38)in.)
Actual measurement: 105(110, 115)cm. (41¼(43¼, 45¼)in.)
Length from shoulder: 68(69, 70)cm. (26¾(27¼, 27½)in.)
Sleeve seam: 49cm. (19¼in.)
Figures in brackets refer to the larger sizes. Where only one figure is given this refers to all sizes.

ABBREVIATIONS

k. knit; *p.* purl; *st(s).* stitch(es); *cm.* centimetres; *mm.* millimetres; *in.* inches; *g.* grammes; *st.st.* stocking stitch; *inc.* increase; *dec.* decrease; *beg.* beginning; *cont.* continue; *foll.* following; *rem.* remaining; *RS.* right side; *WS.* wrong side; *rep.* repeat; *patt.* pattern.

NOTE

When reading chart, work k. rows (odd numbered rows) from right to left and p. rows (even numbered rows) from left to right. Use separate balls of yarn for each colour area worked, twisting yarns together on wrong side at joins to avoid making holes.

INSTRUCTIONS

BACK

With 5½mm. needles and cream, cast on 74(78, 82) sts., and work in k.1, p.1, rib for 6cm. (2¼in.), working an inc. in centre of last row worked – 75(79, 83) sts.
Change to 6mm. needles, and starting with a k. row work in st.st. from appropriate chart for size required as follows:

PLACE CHART

Row 1 (RS): K.1 in cream, now rep. the 36(38, 40) st. patt. twice, work 2 sts. beyond line as shown.
Row 2: Work 2 sts. before line as shown,

now rep. the 36(38, 40) st. patt. twice, p.1 in cream.
Cont. to follow appropriate chart for size required until row 74(78, 82) has been completed.
Now cont. in st.st. in cream only until back measures 68(69, 70)cm. (26¾(27¼, 27½)in.) from cast-on edge, ending with a WS row.

SHAPE SHOULDERS

Cast off 12(13, 14) sts. at beg. of next 4 rows.
Cast off rem. 27 sts.

LEFT FRONT

With 5½mm. needles and cream, cast on 38(40, 42) sts., and work in k.1, p.1, rib for 6cm. (2¼in.) working an inc. in centre of last row worked – 39(41, 43) sts.
Change to 6mm. needles, and starting with a k. row work in st.st. from appropriate chart for size required, working as for back, but working the 36(38, 40) st. patt. once across row.
Cont. as set until row 62(66, 70) has been completed, thus ending with a WS row.

SHAPE FRONT NECK

Keeping patt. correct until chart has been completed, *at the same time,* dec. 1 st. at neck edge on next row and then at this edge on every foll. 4th row until 24(26, 28) sts. remain.
Now cont. straight in cream only until front measures the same as back to beg. of shoulder shaping, ending at side edge.

SHAPE SHOULDER

Cast off 12(13, 14) sts. at beg. of next row.
Work 1 row.
Cast off rem. 12(13, 14) sts.

RIGHT FRONT

Work as for Left Front reversing all shapings.

SLEEVES
(make 2)

With 5½mm. needles and cream, cast on 34(34, 38) sts., and work in k.1, p.1, rib for 7cm. (2¾in.), working 8 incs. evenly spaced along last row worked – 42(42, 46) sts.
Change to 6mm. needles, and starting with a k. row work in st.st., inc. 1 st. at each end of 3rd row and then every foll. 4th row until there are 76(76, 82) sts. on the needle.
Now work straight until sleeve measures 49cm. (19¼in.) from cast-on edge (or length required), ending with a WS row.
Cast off all sts. fairly loosely.

POCKET LININGS
(make 2)

With 6mm. needles and cream, cast on 24 sts., and starting with a k. row work in st.st. for 50 rows.
Cast off fairly loosely.

FRONT BAND

Join both shoulder seams.
With 5½mm. needles and cream, cast on 10 sts., and work in k.1, p.1, rib for 6 rows.
** *Buttonhole row (RS):* Rib 4, cast off 2 sts., rib 4.
Next row: Rib 4, cast on 2 sts., rib 4.
Rib 12 more rows.
Cont. to rep. from ** until 5 buttonholes have been completed. Now cont. straight in rib until band, when slightly stretched, fits up right front, around back neck and down left front, sewing in position as you go along.
Cast off fairly loosely ribwise.

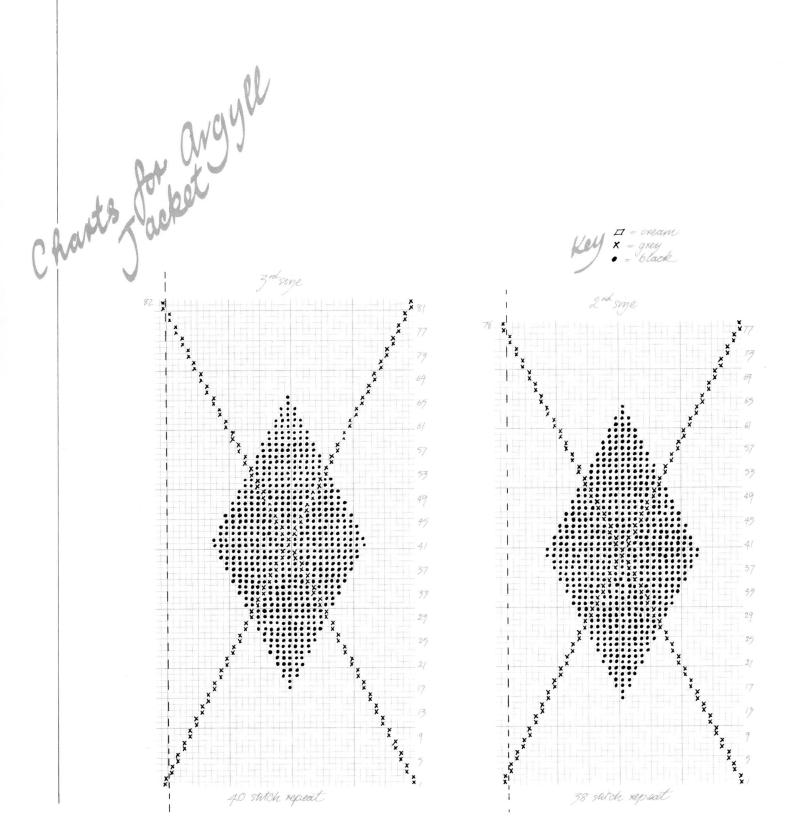

Charts for Argyll Jacket

Key ◻ = cream
X = grey
● = black

3rd size

2nd size

40 stitch repeat

38 stitch repeat

ARGYLL SWEATER

ARGYLL SWEATER WITH SMALL DIAMOND PATTERN
IN CHUNKY YARN

MAKING UP

With centre of cast-off edges of sleeves to shoulder seams, sew sleeves carefully in position, reaching down to same depth on front and back. Leaving an opening of 14cm. (5½in.) in each side seam for pocket, join remainder of side and sleeve seams. Join cast-off and cast-on edges of each pocket then sew row ends to side edges on main part, then join row ends at other end of pocket. Sew on toggles or buttons to correspond with buttonholes. Press seams.

MATERIALS

14(15, 16) 50 g. balls Emu Supermatch Chunky in cream; 2(2, 2) balls in black; 1(1, 1) ball in grey; a pair each 4mm. (no. 8) and 5mm. (no. 6) knitting needles; 2 spare needles.
The quantities of yarn given are based on average requirements and are therefore approximate.

TENSION

15 sts. and 19 rows to 10cm. (4in.) on 5mm. needles over st.st.

MEASUREMENTS

To fit chest: 102(107, 112)cm. (40(42, 44)in.)
Actual measurement: 118(124, 129)cm. (46½(48¾, 50¾)in.)
Length from shoulder: 67(68, 69)cm. (26½(26¾, 27¼)in.)
Sleeve seam: 52(53, 54)cm. (20½(21, 21¼)in.)
Figures in brackets refer to the larger sizes. Where only one figure is given this refers to all sizes.

ABBREVIATIONS

k. knit; **p.** purl; **st(s).** stitch(es); **inc.** increase; **patt.** pattern; **foll.** following; **cont.** continue; **dec.** decrease; **rem.** remaining; **cm.** centimetres; **mm.** millimetres; **in.** inches; **g.** grammes; **RS.** right side; **WS.** wrong side; **st.st.** stocking stitch; **rep.** repeat; **tog.** together.

NOTE

When reading chart, work k. rows (odd numbered rows) from right to left and p. rows (even numbered rows) from left to right. Use separate balls of yarn for each colour area worked, twisting yarns together on wrong side at joins to avoid making holes.

BACK

With 4mm. needles and cream, cast on 81(85, 89) sts., and work in single rib as follows:
Row 1 (RS): K.1, * p.1, k.1, rep. from * to end.
Row 2: P.1, * k.1, p.1, rep. from * to end.
Rep. last 2 rows until rib measures 8cm. (3in.), ending with a 2nd row and working 8 incs. evenly spaced along last row – 89(93, 97) sts.
Change to 5mm. needles and starting with a k. row work in st.st. from chart as follows:

PLACE CHARTS

Row 1 (RS): K.14(16, 18) in cream, now work across the 21 sts. of row 1 of chart, k.19 in cream, now work across the 21 sts. of row 1 of chart, k.14(16, 18) in cream.
Row 2: P.14(16, 18) in cream, now work across the 21 sts. of row 2 of chart, p.19 in cream, now work across the 21sts. of row 2 of chart, p.14(16, 18) in cream.
Cont. as set until the 40 rows of chart are completed. Then rep. these 40 rows as required until back measures 65(66, 67)cm. (25½(26, 26½)in.) from cast-on edge, ending with a WS row.

1st size

36 stitch repeat

SHAPE BACK NECK

Next row: Patt. 28(30, 32), k.2 tog., turn, and work on this first set of sts. only.

** Keeping patt. correct, dec. 1 st. at neck edge on the next 3 rows, thus ending at side edge.

Cast off rem. 26(28, 30) sts.

Return to rem. sts. and slip centre 29 sts. onto a spare needle, with RS facing rejoin yarn to rem. sts., k.2 tog., and patt. to end of row.

Work 1 row.

Now work as for first side from ** to end.

FRONT

Work as for back until front measures 58(59, 60)cm. (22¾(23¼, 23¾)in.) from cast-on edge, ending with a WS row.

SHAPE FRONT NECK

Next row: Patt. 36(38, 40), turn, and work on this first set of sts. only.

*** Keeping patt. correct, dec. 1 st. at neck edge on every row until 26(28, 30) sts. remain.

Now cont. straight until front measures the same as back to cast-off shoulder edge, ending at side edge.

Cast off all sts.

Return to rem. sts., and slip centre 17 sts. onto a spare needle, with RS facing rejoin yarn to rem. sts. and patt. to end of row.

Now work as for first side from *** to end.

SLEEVES
(make 2)

With 4mm. needles and cream, cast on 39(39, 43) sts., and work in single rib as for back welt for 7cm. (2¾in.), ending with a 2nd row and working 4 incs. evenly spaced along last row – 43(43, 47) sts.

Change to 5mm. needles, and starting with a k. row work in st.st., inc. 1 st. at each end of 2nd row and then every foll. 4th row until there are 71(71, 75) sts. on the needle.

Now cont. straight until sleeve measures 52(53, 54)cm. (20½(21, 21¼)in.) from cast-on edge, ending with a WS row.

Cast off all sts. fairly loosely.

NECKBAND

Join right shoulder seam.

With 4mm. needles and cream and RS facing, pick up and k. 19 sts. down left front neck, k. across the 17 sts. at centre front, pick up and k. 20 sts. up right front neck, 6 sts. down right back neck, k. across the 29 sts. at back neck, then pick up and k. 6 sts. up left back neck – 97 sts.

Starting with a 2nd row work in single rib as back welt for 21 rows.

Cast off fairly loosely ribwise.

MAKING UP

Join left shoulder seam and neckband. Fold neckband in half to inside and slip stitch neatly in position. With centre of cast-off edges of sleeves to shoulder seams, sew sleeves carefully in position reaching down to same depth on front and back. Join side and sleeve seams. Press all seams.

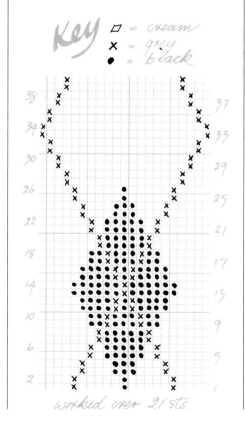

Key □ = cream
× = grey
● = black

worked over 21 sts.

CHENILLE CABLES

CLASSIC V-NECKED CABLED SWEATER IN CHENILLE

MATERIALS

8(9, 9, 10) 100 g. hanks Rowan Cotton Chenille in cream; a pair each 4½mm. (no. 7) and 5½mm. (no. 5) knitting needles; a cable needle; spare needle.
The quantities of yarn given are based on average requirements and are therefore approximate.

TENSION

14 sts. and 22 rows to 10cm. (4in.) on 5½mm. needles over st.st.

MEASUREMENTS

To fit chest: 97(102, 107, 112)cm. (38(40, 42, 44)in.)
Actual measurement: 107(124, 141, 159)cm. (42(49, 55½, 63)in.)
Length from shoulder: 67(69, 71, 73)cm. (26½(27, 28, 28¾)in.)
Sleeve seam (with cuff turned down): 55cm. (21¾in.)
Figures in brackets refer to the larger sizes. Where only one figure is given this refers to all sizes.

ABBREVIATIONS

k. knit; *p.* purl; *st(s).* stitch(es); *inc.* increase; *C4F.* slip next 4 sts. onto cable needle and hold at front of work, k.4, then k.4 from cable needle; *beg.* beginning; *rep.* repeat; *foll.* following; *cont.* continue; *alt.* alternate; *dec.* decrease; *cm.* centimetres; *g.* grammes; *mm.* millimetres; *in.* inches; *RS.* right side; *WS.* wrong side; *st.st.* stocking stitch; *patt.* pattern; *rem.* remaining.

BACK

With 4½mm. needles, cast on 72(82, 92, 102) sts., and work in k.1, p.1, rib for 7cm. (2¾in.) working 18(20, 22, 24) incs. evenly spaced along last row – 90(102, 114, 126) sts.
Change to 5½mm. needles, and work in pattern as follows:
Row 1 (RS): P.5, * k.8, p.4, rep. from * to last 13 sts., k.8, p.5.
Row 2: K.5, * p.8, k.4, rep. from * to last 13 sts., p.8, k.5.
Rep. last 2 rows 3 times more.
Row 9: P.5, * C4F, p.4, rep. from * to last 13 sts., C4F, p.5.
Row 10: As 2nd row.
These 10 rows form the pattern and are repeated throughout.
Cont. straight in patt. until the 9th complete patt. has been worked (90 patt. rows) thus ending with a WS row.

SHAPE ARMHOLES

Keeping patt. correct, cast off 2 sts. at beg. of next 2 rows – 86(98, 110, 122) sts. **
Now cont. straight in patt. until the 2nd(6th, 2nd, 6th) row of the 14th(14th, 15th, 15th) patt. has been worked (132(136, 142, 146) patt. rows) thus ending with a WS row.

SHAPE SHOULDERS

Keeping patt. correct, cast off 7(8, 9, 10) sts. at beg. of next 6 rows, and 6(6, 7, 7) sts. at beg. of foll. 2 rows.
Leave rem. 32(38, 42, 48) sts. on a spare needle.

FRONT

Work as for back to **.

SHAPE V NECK

Next row (RS): Patt. 43(49, 55, 61), turn, and cont. on this first set of sts. only.
*** Keeping patt. correct, dec. 1 st. at beg. (neck edge) on next row and at this edge on every foll. alt. row until 27(30, 34, 37)sts. remain.
Cont. straight until front measures the same as back to beg. of shoulder shaping, ending at armhole edge.

SHAPE SHOULDER

Keeping patt. correct, cast off 7(8, 9, 10) sts. at beg. of next row and foll. 2 alt. rows.
Work 1 row.

Cast off rem. 6(6, 7, 7) sts.
With RS facing rejoin yarn to rem. 43(49, 55, 61) sts. and patt. to end of row.
Now work as for first side from *** to end.

SLEEVES
(make 2)

With 4½mm. needles, cast on 44(44, 52, 52) sts., and work in k.1, p.1, rib for 14cm. (5½in.), working 10(10, 14, 14) incs. evenly spaced across last row – 54(54, 66, 66) sts.
Change to 5½mm. needles, and work in patt. as set for back, *at the same time*, inc. 1 st. at each end of 5th row and then foll. 5th(5th, 4th, 4th) row until there are 74(84, 94, 104) sts. on the needle, working inc. sts. into the patt. on either side.
Now cont. straight until the 9th complete patt. from beg. has been worked (90 patt. rows).
Cast off all sts. fairly loosely.
Measure down 1.5cm. (¾in.) from cast-off edge, and place coloured markers at each side edge.

NECKBAND

Join right shoulder seam.
With 4½mm. needles and RS facing, pick up and k. 42(46, 52, 56) sts. down left side of front neck, pick up and k. 1 st. from centre of V neck and mark this st. with a coloured thread, pick up and k.42(46, 52, 56) sts. up right side of front neck, then work in k.1, p.1, rib over the 32(38, 42, 48) sts. of back neck – 117(131, 147, 161) sts.
Work in k.1, p.1, rib, but dec. 1 st. at each side of the marked centre front st. on every row until 9 rib rows have been completed.
Cast off ribwise, dec. either side of centre marked st. as before.

MAKING UP

Join left shoulder seam and neckband. With centre of cast-off edges of sleeves to shoulder seams, and matching sts. above markers to cast-off sts. at underarm, sew sleeves carefully into armholes. Join side and sleeve seams, reversing seam at cuff for turn back.

BOBBLES & WAVES

ARAN SWEATER WITH BOBBLE AND WAVE CABLE AND HONEYCOMB PATTERN

MATERIALS

15(16) 50 g. balls Emu Superwash D.K. in blue; a pair each 3¾mm. (no. 9) and 4mm. (no. 8) knitting needles; a cable needle; 5 blue buttons; 2 spare needles. *The quantities of yarn given are based on average requirements and are therefore approximate.*

TENSION

20 sts. and 28 rows to 10cm. (4in.) on 4mm. needles over st.st.

MEASUREMENTS

To fit bust: 87–91(91–97)cm. (34–36(36–38)in.)
Actual measurement: 100(116)cm. (39½(45¾)in.)
Length from shoulder: 69(71)cm. (27(28)in.)
Sleeve seam: 54cm. (21¼in.)
Figures in brackets refer to the larger size. Where only one figure is given this refers to both sizes.

ABBREVIATIONS

k. knit; *p.* purl; *st(s).* stitch(es); *inc.* increase; *dec.* decrease; *WS.* wrong side; *RS.* right side; *patt.* pattern; *rep.* repeat; *T3B.* slip next st. onto cable needle and hold at back of work, k.2 then p.1 from cable needle; *T3F.* slip next 2 sts. onto cable needle and hold at front of work, p.1 then k.2 from cable needle; *C3B.* slip next 3 sts. onto cable needle and hold at back of work, k.3 then k.3 from cable needle; *T5F.* slip next 3 sts. onto cable needle and hold at front of work, p.2 then k.3 from cable needle; *T5B.* slip next 2 sts. onto cable needle and hold at back of work, k.3 then p.2 from cable needle; *mb.* with WS facing, k. into front, back and front of next st., (turn and k.3) 3 times, then turn and sl.1, k.2 tog., psso; *C2B.* slip next 2 sts. onto cable needle and hold at back of work, k.2 then k.2 from cable needle; *C2F.* slip next 2 sts. onto cable needle and hold at front of work, k.2 then k.2 from cable needle; *sl.* slip; *tog.* together; *psso.* pass slipped st. over; *g.* grammes; *cm.* centimetres; *mm.* millimetres; *in.* inches; *D.K.* double knitting; *st.st.* stocking stitch; *cont.* continue; *beg.* beginning; *foll.* following; *alt.* alternate; *rem.* remaining.

PATTERN A

(Honeycomb Pattern – worked over 8 sts.)

Row 1 (RS): * C2B., C2F., rep. from * to end.

Rows 2, 4 and 6: P.

Row 3: K.

Row 5: * C2F., C2B., rep. from * to end.

Row 7: K.

Row 8: P.

These 8 rows form **Patt. A** and are repeated as required.

PATTERN B

(Bobbles and Waves – middle panel – worked over 26 sts.)

Row 1 (RS): P.2, T3B., p.5, C3B., p.5, T3F., p.2.

Row 2: K.2, p.2, k.6, p.6, k.6, p.2, k.2.

Row 3: P.1, T3B., p.4, T5B., T5F., p.4, T3F., p.1.

Row 4: K.1, p.2, k.5, p.3, k.4, p.3, k.5, p.2, k.1.

Row 5: T3B., p.3, T5B., p.4, T5F., p.3, T3F.

Row 6: P.2, k.1, mb., k.2, p.3, k.8, p.3, k.2, mb., k.1, p.2.

Row 7: T3F., p.3, k.3, p.8, k.3, p.3, T3B.

Row 8: K.1, p.2, k.3, p.3, k.8, p.3, k.3, p.2, k.1.

Row 9: P.1, T3F., p.2, T5F., p.4, T5B., p.2, T3B., p.1.

Row 10: K.2, p.2, (k.4, p.3) twice, k.4, p.2, k.2.

Row 11: P.2, T3F., p.3, T5F., T5B., p.3, T3B., p.2.

Row 12: K1, mb., k.1, p.2, k.5, p.6, k.5, p.2, k.1, mb., k.1.

These 12 rows form **Patt. B** and are repeated as required.

BACK

With 3¾mm. needles, cast on 130(142) sts. and work in double rib as follows:

Row 1 (RS): K.2, * p.2, k.2, rep. from * to end.

Row 2: P.2, * k.2, p.2, rep. from * to end.

Rep. last 2 rows until rib measures 9cm. (3½in.), ending with a 2nd row and working 21(25) incs. evenly spaced along last row – 151(167) sts.

Change to 4mm. needles, and place patterns as follows:

Row 1 (RS): Patt. over the first 48(56) sts.

by repeating 1st row of *Patt. A* 6(7) times, now patt. over the middle 55 sts. by working 1st row of *Patt. B*, p.3, then work 1st row of *Patt. B*, now patt. over the last 48(56) sts. by working 1st row of *Patt. A* 6(7) times.

Row 2: Patt. over the first 48(56) sts. by working 2nd row of *Patt. A* 6(7) times, now patt. over the middle 55 sts. by working 2nd row of *Patt. B*, k.3, then work 2nd row of *Patt. B*, now patt. over the last 48(56) sts. by working 2nd row of *Patt. A* 6(7) times.

The patts. are now placed **. Cont. to rep. the various pattern rows as required until back measures 66(68)cm. (26(26¾)in.) from cast-on edge, ending with a WS row.

SHAPE BACK NECK

Next row: Patt. 50(58), k.2 tog., turn, and work on this first set of sts. only.

*** Keeping patts. correct, dec. 1 st. at neck edge on every row until 44(52) sts. remain, thus ending at side edge.

SHAPE SHOULDER

Keeping patts. correct, cast off 16 sts. at beg. of next row and foll. alt. row.

Work 1 row.

Cast off rem. 12(20) sts.

Return to rem. sts., and slip centre 47 sts. onto a spare needle.

With RS facing rejoin yarn to rem. sts. K.2 tog. and patt. to end of row.

Work 1 row.

Now work as for first side from *** to end.

FRONT

Work as for back to **.

Now cont. straight in patts. until front measures 59(61)cm. (23¼(24)in.) from cast-on edge, ending with a WS row.

SHAPE FRONT NECK

Next row: Patt. 60(68), turn, and work on this first set of sts. only.

**** Keeping patts. correct, dec. 1 st. at neck edge on every row until 44(52) sts. remain.

Now cont. straight in patts. until front measures the same as back to beg. of shoulder shaping, ending at side edge.

SHAPE SHOULDER

Work as for back shoulder.

Return to rem. sts., and slip centre 31 sts. onto a spare needle.

With RS facing rejoin yarn to rem. sts. and patt. to end of row.

Work 1 row.

Now work as for first side from **** to end.

SLEEVES

(make 2)

With 3¾mm. needles, cast on 66(74) sts., and work in double rib as for back welt for 7cm. (2¾in.), ending with a 2nd row and working 14 incs. evenly spaced along last row – 80(88) sts.

Change to 4mm. needles, and starting with 1st row, rep. the 8 st. patt. of *Patt. A* 10(11) times across row.

Cont. to work sleeves in **Patt. A** only, *at the same time*, inc. 1 st. at each end of every foll. 4th row until there are 144(152) sts. on the needle, working incs. sts. into the patt. at either side.

Now work a few rows straight until sleeve measures 54cm. (21¼in.) from cast-on edge, ending with a WS row.

Cast off all sts. fairly loosely.

NECKBAND

Join right shoulder seam.

With 3¾mm. needles and RS facing, pick up and k. 28 sts. down left front neck edge, work over the 31 sts. of front neck in k.2, p.2, rib working 3 decs. over these 31 sts. (28 sts.), pick up and k. 28 sts. up right front neck edge, 6 sts. down right back neck, work over the 47 sts. of back neck in k.2, p.2, rib. working 3 decs. over these sts. (44 sts.), then pick up and k. 6 sts. up left back neck – 140 sts.

Work in k.2, p.2, rib for 22 rows.

Cast off fairly loosely ribwise.

MAKING UP

Join left shoulder and neckband seam. Fold neckband in half to inside and carefully stitch in position. With centre of cast-off edges of sleeves to shoulder seams, sew sleeves carefully in position reaching down to same depth on front and back.

Join side and sleeve seams.

Sew on buttons as shown. Press all seams.

HOLLOW OAK & LORGNETTE

V-NECKED ARAN JACKET WITH HOLLOW OAK PATTERN AND LORGNETTE CABLES

MATERIALS

20(21) 50 g. balls Emu Supermatch Chunky in off-white; a pair each 4½mm. (no. 7) and 5½mm. (no. 5) knitting needles; a cable needle; 6 buttons; 2 spare needles; 2 stitch holders.
The quantities of yarn given are based on average requirements and are therefore approximate.

TENSION

16 sts. and 22 rows to 10cm. (4in.) on 5½mm. needles over st.st.

MEASUREMENTS

To fit bust: 82-87(91-97)cm. (32-34(36-38)in.)
Length from shoulder: 65cm. (25½in.)
Sleeve seam: 43(45)cm. (17(17¾)in.)
Figures in brackets refer to the larger size. Where only one figure is given this refers to both sizes.

ABBREVIATIONS

BC. sl. next 2 sts. onto cable needle and hold at back of work, k.2, then p.2 from cable needle; *BCK.* sl. next 2 sts. onto cable needle and hold at back of work, k.2 then k.2 from cable needle; *beg.* beginning; *C4F.* sl. next 2 sts. onto cable needle and hold at front of work, k.2 then k.2 from cable needle; *C6F.* sl. next 3 sts. onto cable needle and hold at front of work, k.3 then k.3 from cable needle; *cont.* continue; *dec.* decrease; *FC.* sl. next 2 sts. onto cable needle and hold at front of work, p.2 then k.2 from cable needle; *foll.* following; *inc.* increase; *k.* knit; *MK.* (k.1, p.1) 3 times into next st. then sl. 2nd, 3rd, 4th, 5th and 6th sts. over 1st st. and off right needle; *p.* purl; *patt.* pattern; *rem.* remaining; *rep.* repeat; *RS.* right side; *SBC.* sl. next st. onto cable needle and hold at back of work, k.2 then p.1 from cable needle; *SFC.* sl. next 2 sts. onto cable needle and hold at front of work, p.1 then k.2 from cable needle; *sl.* slip; *st(s).* stitch(es); *st.st.* stocking stitch; *tog.* together; *WS.* wrong side; *cm.* centimetres; *mm.* millimetres; *in.* inches; *g.* grammes.

PANEL A

(worked over 15 sts.)

Row 1 (WS): k.5, p.5, k.5.
Row 2: P.5, k.2, MK., k.2, p.5.
Row 3: As row 1.
Row 4: P.5, MK., k.3, MK., p.5.
Row 5: As row 1.
Row 6: As row 2.
Row 7: As row 1.
Row 8: P.4, SBC., p.1, SFC., p.4.
Row 9: K.4, p.2, k.1, p.1, k.1, p.2, k.4.
Row 10: P.3, SBC., k.1, p.1, k.1, SFC., p.3.
Row 11: K.3, p.3, k.1, p.1, k.1, p.3, k.3.
Row 12: P.2, SBC., (p.1, k.1) twice, p.1, SFC., p.2.
Row 13: K.2, p.2, (k.1, p.1) 3 times, k.1, p.2, k.2.
Row 14: P.2, k.3, (p.1, k.1) twice, p.1, k.3, p.2.
Row 15: As row 13.
Row 16: P.2, SFC., (p.1, k.1) twice, p.1, SBC., p.2.
Row 17: As row 11.
Row 18: P.3, SFC., k.1, p.1, k.1, SBC., p.3.
Row 19: As row 9.
Row 20: P.4, SFC., p.1, SBC., p.4.
These 20 rows form *Panel A*, and are repeated as required.

PANEL B

(worked over 12 sts.)

Row 1 (WS): K.2, p.2, k.4, p.2, k.2.
Row 2: P.2, k.2, p.4, k.2, p.2.
Row 3: As row 1.
Row 4: P.2, FC., BC., p.2.
Row 5: K.4, p.4, k.4.
Row 6: P.4, FC., p.4.
Row 7: K.4, p.2, k.6.
Row 8: P.6., SFC., p.3.
Row 9: K.3, p.2, k.7.
Row 10: P.7, SFC., p.2.
Row 11: K.2, p.2, k.8.
Row 12: P.3, MK., p.4, k.2, p.2.
Row 13: As row 11.
Row 14: P.7, SBC., p.2.
Row 15: As row 9.
Row 16: P.6, SBC., p.3.
Row 17: As row 7.
Row 18: P.4, BCK., p.4.
Row 19: As row 5.
Row 20: P.2, BC., FC., p.2.
Rows 21-25: As rows 1-5.
Row 26: P.4, BC., p.4.
Row 27: K.6, p.2, k.4.
Row 28: P.3, SBC., p.6.
Row 29: K.7, p.2, k.3.

Row 30: P.2, SBC., p.7.
Row 31: K.8, p.2, k.2.
Row 32: P.2, k.2, p.4, MK., p.3.
Row 33: As row 31.
Row 34: P.2, SFC., p.7.
Row 35: As row 29.
Row 36: P.3, SFC., p.6.
Row 37: As row 27.
Row 38: P.4, C4F., p.4.
Row 39: As row 5.
Row 40: As row 20.
These 40 rows form *Panel B*, and are repeated as required.

BACK

With 4½mm. needles, cast on 110(122) sts., and work in double rib as follows:
Row 1 (RS): K.2, * p.2, k.2, rep. from * to end.
Row 2: P.2, * k.2, p.2, rep. from * to end.
Rep. last 2 rows until 12 rows have been worked in all.

Increase row: (Inc. in next st., rib 3, inc. in next st., rib 3(4)) 13 times, inc. in next st., rib 3, inc. in next st., rib 1(0) – 138(150) sts.
Change to 5½mm. needles, and place pattern as follows:
Row 1 (WS): K.0(2), p.0(4), work 1st row of *Panel A* over next 15 sts., p.4, work 1st row of *Panel B* over next 12 sts., p.4, work 1st row of *Panel A* over next 15 sts., p.4, work 1st row of *Panel B* over next 12 sts., p.6, work 1st row of *Panel B* over next 12 sts., p.4, work 1st row of *Panel A* over next 15 sts., p.4, work 1st row of *Panel B* over next 12 sts., p.4, work 1st row of *Panel A* over next 15 sts., p.0(4), k.0(2).
Row 2: P.0(2), k.0(4), work 2nd row of *Panel A* over next 15 sts., k.4, work 2nd row of *Panel B* over next 12 sts., k.4, work 2nd row of *Panel A* over next 15 sts., k.4, work 2nd row of *Panel B* over next 12 sts., k.6, work 2nd row of *Panel B* over next 12 sts., k.4, work 2nd row of *Panel A* over next 15 sts., k.4, work 2nd row of *Panel B* over next 12 sts., k.4, work 2nd row of *Panel A* over next 15 sts., k.0(4), p.0(2).
Row 3: As row 1, but working row 3 of panels.
Row 4: As row 2 but working row 4 of panels and working C4F. in place of k.4, and C6F. in place of k.6.
Rows 5-20: Rep. rows 1-4 four times but working rows 5-20 of panels.
Rows 21-40: As rows 1-20 but work rows 21-40 of *Panel B*.

These 40 rows form the patt. Cont. straight until a total of 137 rows of patt. have been worked from top of rib, thus ending with a 17th patt. row.

SHAPE BACK NECK

Next row (RS): Patt. 47(53), turn, and work on this first set of sts. only.

** Keeping patt. correct, dec. 1 st. at neck edge on next 3 rows, thus ending at side edge – 44(50) sts.

SHAPE SHOULDER

Keeping patt. correct, cast off 22(25) sts. at beg. of next row. Patt. 1 row. Cast off rem. 22(25) sts.

With RS facing, rejoin yarn to rem. sts. and working k.2 tog. each time, cast off centre 44 sts., patt. to end – 47(53) sts. Patt. 1 row.

Now work as for first side from ** to end.

POCKET LININGS
(make 2)

With 5½mm. needles, cast on 26 sts., and starting with a k. row work 26 rows in st.st. Break off yarn and leave sts. on a spare needle.

LEFT FRONT

With 4½mm. needles, cast on 48(54) sts., and work 12 rows in double rib as for back welt, on *1st size* beg. 2nd row, k.2.

Increase row: Rib 2(0), (inc. in next st., rib 2, inc. in next st., rib 1(2)) 9 times, rib 1(0) – 66(72) sts.

Change to 5½mm. needles, and place pattern as follows:

Row 1 (WS): Work 1st row of *Panel B* over next 12 sts., p.4, work 1st row of *Panel A* over next 15 sts., p.4, work 1st row of *Panel B* over next 12 sts., p.4, work 1st row of *Panel A* over next 15 sts., p.0(4), k.0(2).

Row 2: P.0(2), k.0(4), work 2nd row of *Panel A* over next 15 sts., k.4, work 2nd row of *Panel B* over next 12 sts., k.4, work 2nd row of *Panel A* over next 15 sts., k.4, work 2nd row of *Panel B* over next 12 sts.

These 2 rows set position of patt. for left front. Cont. in patt. to match back until a total of 33 patt. rows have been worked from top of rib.

Pocket Opening row (RS): Patt. 6, sl. next 26 sts. onto a stitch holder, patt. across

sts. of first pocket lining, patt. 34(40) sts. Patt. straight for a further 31 rows, thus a total of 65 patt. rows have been worked from top of rib, thus ending at side edge.

SHAPE FRONT NECK

Keeping patt. correct, dec. 1 st. at end (neck edge) of next row and at same edge on every foll. 3rd row until 44(50) sts. remain. Patt. straight until front measures same as back to beg. of shoulder shaping, ending at side edge.

SHAPE SHOULDER

Work as for back.

RIGHT FRONT

Work to match left front, but when working patt., read each row from end to beg. to reverse position of panels and read pocket opening row from end to beg. to reverse position. Work first front dec. at beg. of row.

SLEEVES
(make 2)
(worked from top edge downwards)

With 5½mm. needles, cast on 106(118) sts., and place pattern as follows:

Row 1 (WS): K.0(2), p.0(4), * work 1st row of *Panel A* over next 15 sts., p.4, work 1st row of *Panel B* over next 12 sts., p.4,

work 1st row of *Panel A* over next 15 sts. *, p.6, rep. from * to *, p.0(4), k.0(2).

Row 2: P.0(2), k.0(4), * work 2nd row of *Panel A* over next 15 sts., k.4, work 2nd row of *Panel B* over next 12 sts., k.4, work 2nd row of *Panel A* over next 15 sts. *, k.6, rep. from * to *, k.0(4), p.0(2).

These 2 rows set position of patt. for sleeves. Cont. in patt. to match back until a total of 16 patt. rows have been worked from beg. Keeping patt. correct, dec. 1 st. at each end of next row and every foll. 3rd row until 66(70) sts. remain. Patt. 10(4) rows straight.

Decrease row: P.3(5), * (p.2 tog.) twice, p.1, rep. from * 11 times more, p.3(5) – 42(46) sts.

Change to 4½mm. needles.

Now work in double rib as for back welt for 18 rows.

Cast off fairly loosely ribwise.

FRONT BAND

Join shoulder seams. With 4½mm. needles, cast on 12 sts. Work 4 rows in k.2, p.2, rib.

** *Buttonhole row (RS):* Rib 5, cast off 2 sts., rib 5.

Next row: Rib 5, cast on 2 sts., rib 5. Rib 12 rows **.

Rep. from ** to ** 4 times more, then work 2 buttonhole rows again. Cont. straight in rib until band, when slightly stretched, fits up right front, around back neck and down left front, sewing in position as you go along. Cast off ribwise.

POCKET TOPS
(work 2)

With 4½mm. needles and RS. facing, work in double rib across sts. on stitch holder, as for back welt, for 6 rows. Cast off ribwise.

MAKING UP

With centre of cast-on edges of sleeves to shoulder seams, sew sleeves carefully in position, reaching down to same patt. row on back and front. Join side and sleeve seams. Sew down pocket linings on WS and sides of pocket tops on RS. Sew on buttons to correspond with buttonholes. Press all seams.

LATTICE

ARAN SWEATER WITH ALLOVER LATTICE PATTERN

MATERIALS

27(31) 50 g. balls Pingouin Sport Laine in cream; a pair each 4½mm. (no. 7) and 5½mm. (no. 5) knitting needles; a cable needle; 2 spare needles.

The quantities of yarn given are based on average requirements and are therefore approximate.

TENSION

28 sts. and 25½ rows to 11cm. (4¼in.) – 2 patt. repeats, on 5½mm. needles.

MEASUREMENTS

To fit chest: 97–101(101–107)cm. (38–40(40–42)in.)
Actual measurement: 121(132)cm. (47½(52)in.)
Length from shoulder: 64(65)cm. (25¼(25½)in.)
Sleeve seam: 51(52)cm. (20(20½)in.)
Figures in brackets refer to the larger size. Where only one figure is given this refers to both sizes.

ABBREVIATIONS

k. knit; *p.* purl; *st(s).* stitch(es); *inc.* increase; *rep.* repeat; *C5B.* slip next 2 sts. onto cable needle and hold at back of work, k.3 then p.2 from cable needle; *C5F.* slip next 3 sts. onto cable needle and hold at front of work, p.2, then k.3 from cable needle; *C6F.* slip next 3 sts. onto cable needle and hold at front of work, k.3 then k.3 from cable needle; *patt.* pattern; *beg.* beginning; *cont.* continue; *foll.* following; *rem.* remaining; *cm.* centimetres; *mm.* millimetres; *in.* inches; *g.* grammes; *RS.* right side; *WS.* wrong side; *tog.* together; *dec.* decrease; *st.st.* stocking stitch.

INSTRUCTIONS

BACK

With 4½mm. needles, cast on 138(150) sts., and work in double rib as follows:
Row 1: K.2, * p.2, k.2, rep. from * to end.
Row 2: P.2, * k.2, p.2, rep. from * to end.
Work a further 16 rows as set.
Increase row: Rib 1(6), * inc. into next st. rib 8(7), rep. from * 15(17) times in all, inc. into next st., rib 1(7) – 154(168) sts.
Change to 5½mm. needles and work in pattern as follows:
Row 1 (RS): * C5F., p.4, C5B.,. rep. from * to end.
Row 2: * K.2, p.3, k.4, p.3, k.2, rep. from * to end.
Row 3: * P.2, C5F., C5B., p.2, rep. from * to end.
Row 4: * K.4, p.6, k.4, rep. from * to end.
Row 5: * P.4, C6F., p.4, rep. from * to end.
Row 6: As row 4.
Row 7: * P.4, k.6, p.4, rep. from * to end.
Row 8: As row 4.
Rep. the last 2 rows 4 times more.
Row 17: As row 5.
Row 18: As row 4.
Row 19: * P.2, C5B., C5F., p.2, rep. from * to end.
Row 20: As row 2.
Row 21: * C5B., p.4, C5F., rep. from * to end.
Row 22: * P.3, k.8, p.3, rep. from * to end.
Row 23: K.3, p.8, * C6F., p.8, rep. from * to last 3 sts., k.3.
Row 24: As row 22.
Row 25: K.3, p.8, * K.6, p.8, rep. from * to last 3 sts., k.3.
Row 26: As row 22.
Rep. the last 2 rows 4 times more.
Row 35: As row 23.
Row 36: As row 22.
These 36 rows form the patt. and are repeated as required.
Work straight in patt. until back measures 64(65)cm. (25¼(25½)in.) from cast-on edge ending with a WS row.

SHAPE SHOULDERS

Keeping patt. correct, cast off 25(28) sts. at beg. of next 4 rows.
Leave rem. 54(56) sts. on a spare needle.

FRONT

Work as given for Back until front measures 57(58) cm. (22½(23)in.) from cast-on edge ending with a WS row.

SHAPE FRONT NECK

Next row: Patt. 60(66), work 2 tog., turn and work on this first set of sts. only.
** Keeping patt. correct, dec. 1 st. at neck edge on every row until 50(56) sts. remain.
Now cont. straight until front measures same as back to beg. of shoulder shaping, ending at side edge.

SHAPE SHOULDER

Keeping patt. correct, cast off 25(28) sts. at beg. of next row. Work 1 row.
Cast off rem. 25(28) sts.
Return to rem. sts. and slip centre 30(32) sts. onto a spare needle, with RS facing, rejoin yarn to rem. sts. work 2 tog., and patt. to end of row.
Now work to match first side from ** to end.

SLEEVES
(make 2)

With 4½mm. needles, cast on 58(66) sts., and work in double rib as for back welt for 14 rows.
Increase row: Rib 3(1), * inc. into next st., rib 1, rep. from * to last 3(1) st(s)., rib 3(1) – 84(98) sts.
Change to 5½mm. needles and work in patt. as for back, *at the same time*, inc. 1 st. at each end of the 29th row and then every foll. 4th row until there are 118(132) sts. on the needle, working inc. sts. in reverse st.st. at sides.
Now cont. straight in patt. until sleeve measures 51(52)cm. (20(20½)in.) from cast-on edge, ending with a WS row.
Cast off loosely.

NECKBAND

Join right shoulder seam.
With 4½mm. needles and RS facing, pick up and k.13 sts. down left front neck, k. across the 30(32) sts. of front neck, pick up and k.13 sts. up right front neck, then k. across the 54(56) sts. of back neck – 110(114) sts.
Starting with a 2nd row, work in double rib as for back welt for 9 rows.
Cast off fairly loosely ribwise.

MAKING UP

Join left shoulder and neckband seam. With centre of cast-off edges of sleeves to shoulder seams, sew sleeves carefully in position, reaching down to same depth on front and back. Join side and sleeve seams. Press all seams.

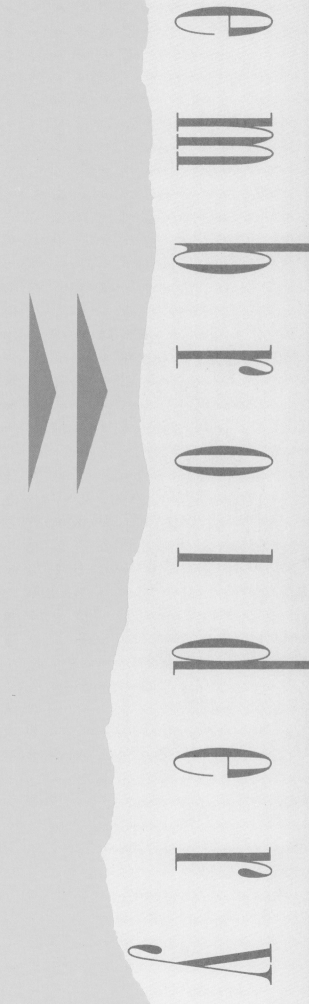

embroidery

CORNFLOWERS & WHEAT

V-NECKED CARDIGAN EMBROIDERED WITH SILVER THREAD, BUGLE BEADS AND SILKS IN CORNFLOWER AND WHEAT DESIGN

MATERIALS

16(18, 20) 25 g. hanks Rowan Light-weight D.K. in pale blue; a pair each 3¼mm. (no. 10) and 3¾mm. (no. 9) knitting needles; a 3¼mm. (no. 10) circular needle; 3 buttons; spare needle.

FOR EMBROIDERY

Stranded Embroidery Cotton in the following colours:

2 skeins light blue; 1 skein each darker blue and gold; 3 spools silver thread; one pack blue bugle beads (long); one pack silver bugle beads (long), and one pack silver bugle beads (short); a beading needle or very thin needle.

The quantities of yarn given are based on average requirements and are therefore approximate.

TENSION

23 sts. and 31 rows to 10cm. (4in.) on 3¾mm. needles over st.st.

MEASUREMENTS

To fit bust: 87(91, 97)cm. (34(36, 38)in.)
Actual measurement: 107(114, 121)cm. (42(45, 47½)in.)
Length from shoulder; 48(50, 52)cm. (19(19¾, 20½)in.)
Sleeve seam: 49cm. (19¼in.)
Figures in brackets refer to the larger sizes. Where only one figure is given this refers to all sizes.

ABBREVIATIONS

k. knit; *p.* purl; *st(s).* stitch(es); *inc.* increase; *alt.* alternate; *beg.* beginning; *cont.* continue; *foll.* following; *rem.* remaining; *RS.* right side; *WS.* wrong side; *st.st.* stocking stitch; *mm.* millimetres; *cm.* centimetres; *in.* inches; *g.* grammes; *D.K.* double knitting; *rep.* repeat; *dec.* decrease; *tog.* together.

BACK

With 3¼mm. needles, cast on 121(129, 137) sts., and work in single rib as follows:
Row 1 (RS): K.1, * p.1, k.1, rep. from * to end.
Row 2: P.1, * k.1, p.1, rep. from * to end.
Rep. last 2 rows until rib measures 6cm. (2½in.), ending with a 2nd row and working an inc. at end of last row – 122(130, 138) sts.
Change to 3¾mm. needles, and starting with a k. row work in st.st. until back measures 29(30, 31)cm. (11½(11¾, 12¼)in.) from cast-on edge, ending with a WS row.

SHAPE ARMHOLES

Cast off 6 sts. at beg. of next 2 rows and 4 sts. at beg. of foll. 2 rows – 102(110, 118) sts.
Now dec. 1 st. at each end of every foll. alt. row until 86(94, 102) sts. remain.
Now work straight until armhole measures 17(18, 19)cm. (6¾(7, 7½)in.) from beg. of shaping, ending with a WS row.

SHAPE BACK NECK

Next row: K.24(28, 32), k.2 tog., turn, and work on this first set of sts. only.
** Dec. 1 st. at neck edge on every row until 20(24, 28) sts. remain, ending at armhole edge.
Cast off rem. sts. fairly loosely.
Return to rem. sts. and slip centre 34 sts. onto a spare needle, with RS facing rejoin yarn to rem. sts., k.2 tog, and k. to end of row.
Work 1 row.
Now work as for first side from ** to end.

LEFT FRONT

With 3¼mm. needles, cast on 59(63, 67) sts., and work in single rib as for back welt for 6cm. (2½in.), ending with a 2nd row and working an inc. at end of last row – 60(64, 68) sts.
Change to 3¾mm. needles, and starting with a k. row work in st.st. until front measures 17(18, 19)cm. (6¾(7, 7½)in.) from cast-on edge, ending with a WS row.

SHAPE FRONT NECK

Dec. 1 st. at neck edge on next row and at this edge on every foll. 4th row until front measures 29(30, 31)cm. (11½(11¾, 12¼)in.) from cast-on edge, ending at side edge.

SHAPE ARMHOLE

Keeping neck decs. as set on every foll. 4th row, *at the same time* at armhole edge, cast off 6 sts. at beg. of next row and 4 sts. on the foll. alt. row. Now dec. 1 st. at same edge on every foll. alt. row 8 times in all.
Now keeping armhole edge straight cont. to dec. at neck edge as set until 20(24, 28) sts. remain.
Now cont. straight until front measures the same as back to cast-off shoulder edge, ending at armhole edge.
Cast off sts. fairly loosely.

RIGHT FRONT

Work as for Left Front, reversing all shapings.

SLEEVES
(make 2)

With 3¼mm. needles, cast on 51(55, 59) sts., and work in single rib as for back welt for 7cm. (2¾in.), ending with a 2nd row and working 15 incs. evenly spaced across last row – 66(70, 74) sts.
Change to 3¾mm. needles, and starting with a k. row work in st.st., inc. 1 st. at each end of every foll. 6th row until there are 92(96, 100) sts. on the needle.
Now cont. straight until sleeve measures 49cm. (19¼in.) from cast-on edge, ending with a WS row.

SHAPE TOP

Cast off 6 sts. at beg. of next 2 rows, and 4 sts. at beg. of foll. 2 rows – 72(76, 80) sts.
Now dec. 1 st. at each end of every row until 20(22, 24) sts. remain.
Cast off 4 sts. at beg. of next 2 rows.
Cast off rem. 12(14, 16) sts.

FRONT BAND

Join both shoulder seams.
With the 3¼mm. circular needle and RS facing, pick up and k. 44 sts. along right front straight edge to beg. of neck shaping, 74(76, 78) sts. along shaped neck edge, 49 sts. along back neck edge (including the 34 sts. on spare needle), pick up and k. 74(76, 78) sts. along shaped neck edge of left front, and 44 sts. along left front straight edge – 285(289, 293) sts.
Starting with a 2nd row, work in single rib as for back welt for 5 rows.
Buttonhole row (RS): Rib 6, * cast off 2 sts., rib 16 (including st. on needle), rep. from * once more, cast off 2 sts., rib to end.
Next row: Rib, casting on 2 sts., over cast-off sts. on previous row.
Rib 2 more rows.
Cast off fairly loosely ribwise.

MAKING UP

With centre of sleeve tops to shoulder seams, sew sleeves carefully into arm- holes stretching slightly to fit. Join side and sleeve seams. Sew on buttons to cor- respond with buttonholes. Press all seams.

chart for left front -

EMBROIDERY INSTRUCTIONS

Transfer design using photo as a guide for placement. Begin by working the bow in chain stitch, using 3 strands of gold. Now work silver leaves and stems in chain stitch, working outwards for leaves. Sew on silver bugle beads to complete wheat stalks, using smaller beads for smaller stalks.

Using 3 strands of light blue, chain stitch cornflower stalks and leaves and work large French knots in dark blue for flower centres. Complete cornflowers by sewing on blue bugle beads. Satin stitch calyxes in dark blue.

reverse for right front

CLOVE CARNATIONS

ROUND-NECKED CARDIGAN WITH CLOVE CARNATION SATIN APPLIQUÉ FLOWERS AND EMBROIDERED LEAVES AND INSECTS

MATERIALS

17(19, 21) 25 g. hanks Rowan Light-weight D.K. in peach; a pair each 3¼mm. (no. 10) and 3¾mm. (no. 9) knitting needles; spare needle; 2 safety pins; 7 pearl buttons.

FOR EMBROIDERY

Stranded Embroidery Cotton in the following colours:
2 skeins light pink; 1 skein each dark pink, pale green, darker green, pale grey and pale blue; remnant of washable pale pink or peach satin or shiny fabric; small amount of lightweight polyester wadding. *The quantities of yarn given are based on average requirements and are therefore approximate.*

TENSION

23 sts. and 31 rows to 10cm. (4in.) on 3¾mm. needles over st.st.

MEASUREMENTS

To fit bust: 87(91, 97)cm. (34(36, 38)in.)
Actual measurement: 101(106, 111)cm. (40(41¾, 43¾)in.)
Length from shoulder: 58(59, 60)in. (23(23¼, 23½)in.)
Sleeve seam: 49cm. (19¼in.)
Figures in brackets refer to the larger sizes. Where only one figure is given this refers to all sizes.

ABBREVIATIONS

k. knit; *p.* purl; *st(s).* stitch(es); *beg.* beginning; *cont.* continue; *dec.* decrease; *foll.* following; *inc.* increase; *rem.* remaining; *RS.* right side; *WS.* wrong side; *st.st.* stocking stitch; *cm.* centimetres; *mm.* millimetres; *in.* inches; *g.* grammes; *D.K.* double knitting; *rep.* repeat.

BACK

With 3¼mm. needles, cast on 111(117, 123) sts., by the thumb method, and work in single rib as follows:

Row 1: K.1, * p.1, k.1, rep. from * to end.
Row 2: P.1, * k.1, p.1, rep. from * to end.
Rep. last 2 rows until 11 rows in all have been worked, working 5 incs. evenly spaced across last row – 116(122, 128) sts.

Change to 3¾mm. needles, and starting with a k. row, work in st.st. until back measures 56(57, 58)cm. (22(22½, 23)in.) from cast-on edge, ending with a WS row.

SHAPE BACK NECK

Next row: K.42(45, 48), turn, and work on this first set of sts. only.
** Dec. 1 st. at neck edge on next 5 rows, thus ending at side edge.
Cast off rem. 37(40, 43) sts.
Return to rem. sts. and slip centre 32 sts. onto a spare needle. With RS facing rejoin yarn to rem. sts., and k. to end of row. Work 1 row.
Now work as for first side from ** to end.

RIGHT FRONT

With 3¼mm. needles, cast on 63(66, 69) sts., by the thumb method, and work in single rib as for back welt for 7 rows.
Buttonhole row (RS): Rib 4, cast off 2 sts., rib to end.
Next row: Rib to last 4 sts., cast on 2 sts., rib 4.
Rib 2 more rows. (11 rib rows worked in all.)
Change to 3¾mm. needles.
Next row (RS): Slip first 10 sts. onto a safety pin, k. across rem. sts. and inc. 3 sts. evenly across – 56(59, 62) sts.
Now starting with a p. row work in st.st. until front measures 49(50, 51)cm. (19¼(19¾, 20)in.) from cast-on edge, ending at centre front edge.

SHAPE FRONT NECK

Cast off 9 sts. at beg. of next row, work to end.
Now dec. 1 st. at neck edge on every row until 37(40, 43) sts. remain.
Now cont. straight until front measures the same as back to cast-off shoulder edge, ending at side edge.
Cast off all. sts.

LEFT FRONT

Work as Right Front, reversing all shapings.

SLEEVES
(make 2)

With 3¼mm. needles, cast on 51(55, 59) sts., by the thumb method, and work in single rib as for back welt for 7cm. (2¾in.), working 15 incs. evenly spaced across last row – 66(70, 74) sts.
Change to 3¾mm. needles, and starting with a k. row, work in st.st., inc. 1 st. at each end of every foll. 6th row until there are 108(112, 116) sts. on the needle.
Now cont. straight until sleeve measures 49cm. (19¼in.) from cast-on edge, ending with a WS row.
Cast off all sts. fairly loosely.

FRONT BANDS

With 3¼mm. needles rejoin yarn to the 10 sts. at right front edge.
Work in rib as set for 6 rows.
* *Buttonhole row (RS):* Rib 4, cast off 2 sts. rib to end.
Next row: Rib 4, cast on 2 sts., rib to end.
Rib 20 rows.
Cont. to rep. from * until the 6th buttonhole has been completed.
Rib 18(19, 20) rows. Sew in position, stretching slightly, as you work.
Leave sts. on a safety pin.
Work the other band to match, but without buttonholes.

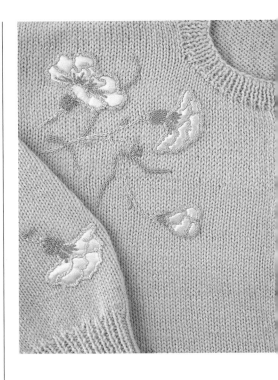

chart for left front

48

NECKBAND

Join both shoulder seams.

With 3¼mm. needles and RS facing, rib across the 10 sts. of buttonhole band, then pick up and k. 40 sts. up right front neck, 6 sts. down right back neck, k. across the 32 sts. at back neck, pick up and k. 6 sts. up left back neck, 40 sts. down left front neck and finally rib across the 10 sts. of button band – 144 sts.

Keeping bands correct, work in k.1, p.1, rib for 1 row.

Rep. the 2 buttonhole rows again.

When 7 rib rows in all have been worked, cast off fairly loosely ribwise.

MAKING UP

With centre of cast-off edges of sleeves to shoulder seams, sew sleeves carefully in position, reaching down to same depth on front and back. Join side and sleeve seams. Sew on buttons to correspond with buttonholes.

EMBROIDERY INSTRUCTIONS

Transfer design, as explained in Knitting Notes. Trace the flower outlines onto tracing paper. Pin to fabric and wadding, flattening slightly with an iron if necessary.

Using sharp scissors, cut round traced outline slightly larger than your tracing. Lightly pencil in all detail.

Tack appliqué shapes to garment using photo as a guide for placement. Neatly blanket stitch each outline with matching thread. Use large french knots for flower outlines and small french knots to delineate petals. Chain stitch stamens, stems and calyxes using 3 strands of pale green and darker green for leaves. Work dragonfly by working chain stitch outwards in spirals for wings with grey. Work large french knots in blue for body.

chart for right front

CABBAGE ROSES

LOOSE ROUND-NECKED SWEATER WITH APPLIQUÉ SATIN ROSES AND EMBROIDERED LEAVES AND STEMS

MATERIALS

19(21, 23) 25 g. hanks Rowan Lightweight D.K. in pale yellow; a pair each 3¼mm. (no. 10) and 3¾mm. (no. 9) knitting needles; 2 spare needles.

FOR EMBROIDERY

Stranded Embroidery Cotton in the following colours:
1 skein in each pale pink, pale beige and pale green; remnant of washable white satin or shiny fabric; small amount of lightweight polyester wadding; a beading needle or very thin needle.
The quantities of yarn given are based on average requirements and are therefore approximate.

TENSION

23 sts. and 31 rows to 10cm. (4in.) on 3¾mm. needles over st.st.

MEASUREMENTS

To fit bust: 87(91, 97)cm. (34(36, 38)in.)
Actual measurement: 113(118, 123)cm. (44½(46½, 48½)in.)
Length from shoulder: 70(71, 72)cm. (27½(28, 28¼)in.)
Sleeve seam: 49cm. (19¼in.)
Figures in brackets refer to the larger sizes. Where only one figure is given this refers to all sizes.

ABBREVIATIONS

k. knit; *p.* purl; *st(s).* stitch(es); *inc.* increase; *dec.* decrease; *foll.* following; *rem.* remaining; *RS.* right side; *WS.* wrong side; *st.st.* stocking stitch; *mm.* millimetres; *cm.* centimetres; *in.* inches; *g.* grammes; *rep.* repeat; *tog.* together; *cont.* continue; *D.K.* double knitting.

BACK

With 3¼mm. needles, cast on 129(135, 141) sts., and work in single rib as follows:
Row 1 (RS): K.1, * p.1, k.1, rep. from * to end.
Row 2: P.1, * k.1, p.1, rep. from * to end.
Rep. last 2 rows until rib measures 7cm. (2¾in.), ending with a 2nd row and working an inc. at end of last row – 130(136, 142) sts.
Change to 3¾mm. needles, and starting with a k. row, work in st.st. until back measures 64(65, 66)cm. (25¼(25½, 26)in.) from cast-on edge, ending with a WS row.

SHAPE BACK NECK

Next row: K.42(45, 48), k.2 tog., turn, and work on this first set of sts. only.
** Dec. 1 st. at neck edge on next 7 rows – 36(39, 42) sts.
Now cont. straight until back measures 70(71, 72)cm. (27½(28, 28¼)in.) from cast-on edge, ending at side edge.
Cast off rem. 36(39, 42) sts.
Return to rem. sts., and slip centre 42 sts. onto a spare needle, with RS facing rejoin yarn to rem. sts., k.2 tog., and k. to end of row.
Work 1 row.
Now work as for first side from ** to end.

FRONT

Work as for back until front measures 52(53, 54)cm. (20½(21, 21¼)in.) from cast-on edge, ending with a WS row.

SHAPE FRONT NECK

Next row: K.47(50, 53), k.2 tog., turn, and work on this first set of sts. only.
*** Dec. 1 st. at neck edge on every row until 36(39, 42) sts. remain.
Now cont. straight until front measures same as back to cast-off shoulder edge, ending at side edge.
Cast off all sts.
Return to rem. sts., and slip centre 32 sts. onto a spare needle, with RS facing rejoin yarn to rem. sts., k.2 tog., and k. to end of row. Work 1 row.
Now work as for first side from *** to end.

SLEEVES
(make 2)

With 3¼mm. needles, cast on 51(55, 59) sts., and work in single rib as for back welt for 7cm. (2¾in.) ending with a 2nd row,

and working 21 incs. evenly spaced across last row – 72(76, 80) sts.

Change to 3¾mm. needles, and starting with a k. row work in st.st., inc. 1 st. at each end of every foll. 4th row 12 times, then at each end of every foll. 3rd row 16 times – 128(132, 136) sts.

Now cont. straight until sleeve measures 49cm. (19¼in.) from cast-on edge, ending with a WS row.

Cast off all sts. fairly loosely.

NECKBAND

Join right shoulder seam.

With 3¼mm. needles and RS facing, pick up and k. 36 sts. down left front neck, k. across the 32 sts. at centre front, working 4 decs. across – 28 sts., now pick up and k. 36 sts. up right front neck, 14 sts. down right back neck, k. across the centre 42 sts. at back neck, working 4 decs. across – 38 sts., then pick up and k. 14 sts. up left back neck – 166 sts.

Work in k.1, p.1, rib for 16 rows.

Cast off fairly loosely ribwise.

MAKING UP

Join left shoulder and neckband seam. With centre of cast-off edges of sleeves to shoulder seams, sew sleeves carefully in position, reaching down to same depth on front and back. Join side and sleeve seams. Press all seams.

EMBROIDERY INSTRUCTIONS

Transfer design as explained in Knitting Notes. Trace the flower outline onto tracing paper, pin to fabric and wadding, flattening slightly with an iron if necessary. Using sharp scissors, cut round traced outline slightly larger than your tracing. Lightly pencil in detail.

Tack appliqué shapes to garment using photo as a guide for placement. Neatly work round each outline in french knots in pale pink (using 3 strands). Work petals inside outline in chain stitch in pale pink. Chain stitch stems in 3 strands of pale beige and work leaves in chain stitch in 3 strands of pale green.

Left half of design – Rose is worked again at centre as shown on photo, then this half is repeated for right half of garment.

HIBISCUS

COTTON SWEATER WITH PICOT EDGING, APPLIQUÉ RED FLOWERS AND EMBROIDERED LEAVES

MATERIALS

5(6, 6) 50 g. balls Pingouin Corrida 3 in ficelle; a pair each 2¾mm. (no. 12) and 3mm. (no. 11) knitting needles; 3 buttons.

FOR EMBROIDERY

Stranded Embroidery Cotton in the following colours:
1 skein each red, pale red, light green and darker green; tiny black beads; black thread; a beading needle or very thin needle; remnant of washable red satin or shiny fabric; small amount of lightweight polyester wadding.

The quantities of yarn given are based on average requirements and are therefore approximate.

TENSION

27 sts. and 33 rows to 10cm. (4in.) on 3mm. needles over st.st.

MEASUREMENTS

To fit bust: 81(87, 91)cm. (32(34, 36)in.)
Actual measurement: 91(96, 101)cm. (36(38, 40)in.)
Length from shoulder: 60(61.5, 63)cm. (23½(24¼, 24¾)in.)

Figures in brackets refer to the larger sizes. Where only one figure is given this refers to all sizes.

ABBREVIATIONS

k. knit; *p.* purl; *st(s).* stitch(es); *rep.* repeat; *beg.* beginning; *tog.* together; *dec.* decrease; *st.st.* stocking stitch; *y.fd.* yarn forward; *mm.* millimetres; *cm.* centimetres; *in.* inches; *g.* grammes; *RS.* right side; *WS.* wrong side; *foll.* following; *cont.* continue; *alt.* alternate.

INSTRUCTIONS

BACK

With 2¾mm. needles, cast on 129(137, 145) sts., and starting with a k. row work 4 rows in st.st.

Picot row (RS): K.1., * y.fd., k.2 tog., rep. from * to end.

Change to 3mm. needles, and starting with a p. row, work in st.st., dec. 1 st. at each end of every foll. 10th row until 121(129, 137) sts. remain.

Now cont. straight until back measures 42cm (16½in.) from picot row, ending with a WS row.

SHAPE ARMHOLES

Cast off 6(7, 8) sts. at beg. of next 2 rows.

Now dec. 1 st. at each end of every row until 81(85, 89) sts. remain.

Work 4(6, 8) rows straight.

SHAPE BACK NECK

Next row (RS): K.26(27, 28), cast off centre 29(31, 33) sts., k. to end of row, and cont. on this last set of sts. only.

** Dec. 1 st. at neck edge on next 10 rows, then dec. 1 st. at this edge on every foll. alt. row until 10(11, 12) sts. remain.

Now cont. straight until back measures 60(61.5, 63)cm. (23½(24¼, 24¾)in.) from picot row, ending with a WS row.

Cast off.

With WS facing rejoin yarn to rem. sts., and work as for first side from ** to end.

FRONT

Work as for back until front measures 37cm. (14½in.) from picot row, ending with a WS row.

FRONT OPENING

Next row: K.60(64, 68), pick up loop lying between needles and k. into back of it, turn, and work on this first set of 61(65, 69) sts. only.

Cont. straight until front measures 42cm. (16½in.) from picot row, ending at side edge.

SHAPE ARMHOLE

Cast off 6(7, 8) sts. at beg. of next row.

Work 1 row. Now dec. 1 st. at armhole edge on every row until 41(43, 45) sts. remain.

Work 5(7, 9) rows straight, thus ending at centre front edge.

SHAPE NECK

Cast off 15(16, 17) sts. at beg. of next row.

Now work as for back from ** to end.

With RS facing rejoin yarn to rem. sts., cast on 1 st.

Now work as for first side reversing all shapings.

EDGINGS

With 2¾mm. needles and RS facing, pick up and k. 28(32, 36) sts. up right side of front opening, 2 sts. from corner and 57(61, 65) sts. around front neck edge to right shoulder – 87(95, 103) sts.

Starting with a p. row work 3 rows in st.st.

Work picot row as hemline of back.

Work 3 more rows in st.st.

Cast off fairly loosely.

Beg. at left shoulder, work left side of neck and front opening in the same way.

Work same edging across back neck, picking up 119(123, 127) sts. between shoulders.

Join both shoulder and picot edging seams.

Work same edging around both armholes, picking up 125(131, 137) sts.

MAKING UP

Join side seams. Fold neck and armhole edgings and lower edging to wrong side at picot rows and catch stitch in position. Lap right picot edging over left at front opening and secure in place with 3 buttons.

chart for right front

EMBROIDERY INSTRUCTIONS

Transfer design, as explained in Knitting Notes. Trace flower outlines onto tracing paper. Pin to fabric and wadding, flattening slightly with an iron, if necessary. Using sharp scissors, cut round trace outline slightly larger than your tracing. Lightly pencil in all detail. Tack appliqué shapes to garment using photo as a guide for placement. Neatly blanket stitch each outline with matching thread. Use large french knots for flower outlines and to delineate petals. Chain stitch leaves and stems, using three strands of green, using light and dark greens as shown, and working in chain stitch, outward in spirals. Sew on small black beads in flower centres with a beading needle.

chart for left front

BUTTERFLY

BLACK EVENING SWEATER WITH LACE BUTTERFLY APPLIQUE, BEADS AND SEQUINS

MATERIALS

17(19, 21) 25 g. hanks Rowan Lightweight D.K. in black; a pair each 3¼mm. (no. 10) and 3¾mm. (no. 9) knitting needles; 2 spare needles.

FOR EMBROIDERY

1 metre (1¼ yards) fine white edging lace, width 14cm. (5½in.); 2 metres (2½ yards) each pearl and silver bead trim (fine); white sewing thread; 1 string iridescent sequins; tiny beads to secure sequins; selection of round and pear shaped stones (available from Ells & Farrier, see Useful Addresses); a beading needle or very thin needle.

The quantities of yarn given are based on average requirements and are therefore approximate.

TENSION

23 sts. and 31 rows to 10cm. (4in.) on 3¾mm. needles over st.st.

MEASUREMENTS

To fit bust: 87(91, 97)cm. (34(36, 38)in.)
Actual measurement: 98(105, 112)cm. (38½(41½, 44)in.)
Length from shoulder: 43(44, 45)cm. (17(17¼, 17¾)in.)
Sleeve seam: 48cm. (19in.)
Figures in brackets refer to the larger sizes. Where only one figure is given this refers to all sizes.

ABBREVIATIONS

k. knit; *p.* purl; *st(s).* stitch(es); *inc.* increase; *dec.* decrease; *st.st.* stocking stitch; *foll.* following; *mm.* millimetres; *cm.* centimetres; *in.* inches; *g.* grammes; *RS.* right side; *WS.* wrong side; *D.K.* double knitting; *rep.* repeat; *tog.* together; *rem.* remaining; *cont.* continue.

BACK

With 3¼mm. needles, cast on 99(107, 115) sts., and work in single rib as follows:
Row 1 (RS): K.1, * p.1, k.1, rep. from * to end.
Row 2: P.1, * k.1, p.1, rep. from * to end.
Rep. last 2 rows until rib measures 8cm. (3in.), ending with a 2nd row and working 14 incs. evenly spaced across last row – 113(121, 129) sts.
Change to 3¾mm. needles, and starting with a k. row work straight in st.st. until back measures 38(39, 40)cm. (15(15¼, 15¾)in.) from cast-on edge, ending with a WS row.

SHAPE BACK NECK

Next row: K.40(44, 48), k.2 tog., turn, and work on this first set of sts. only.
** Dec. 1 st. at neck edge on every row until 28(32, 36) sts. remain.
Work 2 rows in st.st., thus ending at side edge.
Cast off sts. fairly loosely.
Return to rem. sts. and slip centre 29 sts. onto a spare needle, with RS facing rejoin yarn to rem. sts., k.2 tog., and k. to end of row. Work 1 row.
Now work as for first side from ** to end.

FRONT

Work as for back until front measures 36(37, 38)cm. (14¼(14½, 15)in.) from cast-on edge, ending with a WS row.

SHAPE FRONT NECK

Next row: K.40(44, 48), k.2 tog., turn, and work on this first set of sts. only.
*** Dec. 1 st. at neck edge on every row until 28(32, 36) sts. remain.
Now cont. straight until front measures the same as back to cast-off shoulder edge, ending at side edge.
Cast off sts. fairly loosely.
Return to rem. sts. and slip centre 29 sts. onto a spare needle.
With RS facing rejoin yarn to rem. sts., k.2 tog., and k. to end of row. Work 1 row.
Now work as for first side from *** to end.

SLEEVES
(make 2)

With 3¼mm. needles, cast on 47(47, 53) sts., and work in single rib as for back welt for 8cm. (3in.), ending with a 2nd row and working 24 incs. evenly spaced along last row – 71(71, 77) sts.
Change to 3¾mm. needles, and starting with a k. row work in st.st., inc. 1 st. at each end of every foll. 4th row 12 times, then at each end of every foll. 3rd row 16 times – 127(127, 133) sts.
Now cont. straight until sleeve measures 48cm. (19in.) from cast-on edge, ending with a WS row.
Cast off all sts. fairly loosely.

NECKBAND

Join right shoulder seam.
With 3¼mm. needles and RS facing, pick up and k. 30 sts. down left front neck, k. across the 29 sts. at centre front, pick up and k. 30 sts. up right front neck, 18 sts. down right back neck, k. across the 29 sts. at centre back, then pick up and k. 17 sts. up left back neck – 153 sts.
Starting with a 2nd row, work in single rib as for back welt for 7 rows.
Cast off fairly loosely ribwise.

MAKING UP

Join left shoulder and neckband seam. With centre of cast-off edges of sleeves to shoulder seams, sew sleeves carefully in position reaching down to same depth on front and back. Join side and sleeve seams. Press all seams.

EMBROIDERY INSTRUCTIONS

Trace outlines of the butterflies onto thin tracing paper. Pin to lace. Using sharp scissors, cut round the traced outline slightly larger than your tracing. Lightly pencil in detail onto lace. Tack butterflies in position using photo as a guide, one on front and the other at centre of back. Neatly blanket stitch round outline in white thread. Sew on pearl and silver trim where shown, using simple couching (see Knitting Notes). Sew on round and pear shaped stones. Stitch on sequins, securing each with a tiny bead as shown.

chart for back

chart for front

PARMA VIOLETS

ROUND NECKED CARDIGAN WITH CROSS STITCH
(PATTERN CAN ALSO BE WORKED IN FAIR ISLE FROM THE CHART)

MATERIALS
16(18, 20) 25 g. hanks Rowan Light-weight D.K. in violet; a pair each 3¼mm. (no. 10) and 3¾mm. (no. 9) knitting needles; 8 buttons; spare needle; 2 safety pins.

FOR EMBROIDERY
Tapisserie wool, 1 hank in the following colours: pale grey, white, dark purple, peach, medium lilac; 2 hanks in lilac; a tapestry needle.
The quantities of yarn given are based on average requirements and are therefore approximate.

TENSION
23 sts. and 31 rows to 10cm. (4in.) on 3¾mm. needles over st.st.

MEASUREMENTS
To fit bust: 87(91, 97)cm. (34(36, 38)in.)
Actual measurement: 94(101, 108)cm. (37(40, 42½)in.)
Length from shoulder: 58(59, 60)cm. (23(23¼, 23½)in.)
Sleeve seam: 49cm. (19¼in.)
Figures in brackets refer to the larger sizes. Where only one figure is given this refers to all sizes.

ABBREVIATIONS
k. knit; *p.* purl; *st(s).* stitch(es); *dec. 2* slip one st., knit 2 sts. together, pass slipped st. over; *st.st.* stocking stitch; *beg.* beginning; *M1* pick up horizontal loop lying between st. just worked and following st. and work into the back of it; *mm.* millimetres; *cm.* centimetres; *in.* inches; *g.* grammes; *D.K.* double knitting; *RS.* right side; *WS.* wrong side; *rep.* repeat; *inc.* increase; *cont.* continue; *foll.* following; *alt.* alternate; *tog.* together; *dec.* decrease; *rem.* remaining.

BACK

With 3¼mm. needles, cast on 102(110, 118) sts., and work in double rib as follows:

Row 1 (RS): K.2, * p.2, k.2, rep. from * to end.

Row 2: P.2, * k.2, p.2, rep. from * to end.

Rep. last 2 rows until 12 rib rows have been worked in all, working an inc. at each end of last row worked – 104(112, 120) sts.

Change to 3¾mm. needles, and starting with a k. row work in st.st. for 22 rows.

WORK SHAPINGS

Next row (RS): K.26(28, 30), dec. 2, k.46(50, 54), dec. 2, k.26(28, 30).

Starting with a p. row work 5 rows in st.st.

Next row: K.25(27, 29), dec. 2, k.44(48, 52), dec. 2, k.25(27, 29).

Starting with a p. row work in st.st. for 3 rows.

Next row: K.24(26, 28), dec. 2, k.42(46, 50), dec. 2, k.24(26, 28).

Starting with a p. row work in st.st. for 3 rows.

Next row: K.23(25, 27), dec. 2, k.40(44, 48), dec. 2, k.23(25, 27).

Starting with a p. row work in st.st. for 3 rows.

Next row: K.22(24, 26), dec. 2, k.38(42, 46), dec. 2, k.22(24, 26) – 84(92, 100) sts.

Starting with a p. row work in st.st. for 15 rows.

Next row: K.22(24, 26), M1, k. to last 22(24, 26) sts., M1, k.22(24, 26).

Starting with a p. row work in st.st. for 3 rows.

Rep. last 4 rows until there are 104(112, 120) sts. on the needle.

Now cont. straight in st.st. for a further 11 rows from last inc. row, thus ending with a WS row.

SHAPE ARMHOLES

Cast off 6 sts. at beg. of next 2 rows, and 4 sts. at beg. of foll. 2 rows.

Now dec. 1 st. at each end of every foll. alt. row until 80(88, 96) sts. remain.

Now cont. straight until armholes measure 18(19, 20)cm. (7(7½, 8)in.) from beg. of shaping, ending with a WS row.

SHAPE BACK NECK

Next row: K.22(26, 30), k.2 tog., turn, and work on this first set of sts. only.

** Dec. 1 st. at neck edge on every row until 18(22, 26) sts. remain, thus ending with a WS row.

Cast off all sts.

Return to rem. sts. and slip centre 32 sts. onto a spare needle, with RS facing rejoin yarn to rem. sts. k.2 tog., and k. to end of row.

Now work as for first side from ** to end.

LEFT FRONT

With 3¼mm. needles, cast on 54(58, 62) sts., and work in double rib as for back welt for 12 rows.

Change to 3¾mm. needles, and starting with a k. row work in st.st. for 22 rows.

WORK SHAPINGS

Next row (RS): K.26(28, 30), dec. 2, k.25(27, 29).

Cont. shaping as now set, and working as for back until 44(48, 52) sts. remain.

Starting with a p. row work in st.st. for 15 rows.

Next row: K.22(24, 26), M1, k.22(24, 26).

Starting with a p. row work 3 rows in st.st.

Rep. last 4 rows until 54(58, 62) sts. are on the needle.

Now cont. straight in st.st. for a further 11 rows from last inc. row, thus ending with a WS row.

SHAPE ARMHOLE

Cast off 6 sts. at beg. of next row and 4 sts. at beg. of foll. alt. row.

Now dec. 1 st. at same edge on every foll. alt. row until 44(48, 52) sts. remain.

Now cont. straight until armhole measures 12(13, 14)cm. (4¾(5, 5½)in.) from beg. of shaping, ending at centre front edge.

SHAPE FRONT NECK

Cast off 8 sts. at beg. (neck edge) on next row and 5 sts. at beg. of foll. alt. row.

Now dec. 1 st. at neck edge on every row until 18(22, 26) sts. remain.

Now cont. straight until front measures the same as back to cast-off shoulder edge, ending with a WS row.

Cast off all sts.

shoulder seam

Right front

neck shaping

centre front edge

3rd 2nd 1st sizes   44(48, 50) sts.   all sizes
(including one selvedge stitch at each
end of every row)

RIGHT FRONT

Work as for Left Front, reversing all shapings, i.e. begin decs. in shapings as follows:

Next row (RS): K.25(27, 29), dec. 2, k.26(28, 30), and begin incs. in shaping as follows:

Next row: K.22(24, 26), M1, k.22(24, 26).

SLEEVES

(make 2)

With 3¼mm. needles cast on 58(62, 66) sts., and work in double rib as for back welt for 7cm. (2¾in.), working 15 incs. evenly spaced across last row – 73(77, 81) sts.

Change to 3¾mm. needles, and starting with a k. row work in st.st. inc. 1 st. at each end of every foll. 6th row until there are 89(93, 97) sts. on the needle.

Now cont. straight until sleeve measures 49cm. (19¼in.) from cast-on edge, ending with a WS row.

SHAPE TOP

Cast off 6 sts. at beg. of next 2 rows, and 4 sts. at beg. of foll. 2 rows – 69(73, 77) sts. Now dec. 1 st. at each end of every foll. alt. row 10 times then at each end of every row until 21 sts. remain on the needle. Cast off 4 sts. at beg. of next 2 rows, then cast off rem. 13 sts. fairly loosely.

FRONT BANDS

With 3¼mm. needles cast on 12 sts., and work in k.2, p.2, rib for 8 rows.
*Buttonhole row (RS): Rib 5, cast off 2 sts., rib to end.
Next row: Rib 5, cast on 2 sts., rib to end. Rib 20 rows.
Cont. to rep. from * until the 7th buttonhole has been completed.
Rib a further 18(20, 22) rows.
Leave sts. on a safety pin.
Work another band to match, but omit the buttonholes.

NECKBAND

Join both shoulder seams.
With 3¼mm. needles and RS facing, rib over the 12 sts. of buttonhole band, then pick up and k. 36 sts. up right front neck, 10 sts. down right back neck, k. across the 32 sts. at back neck, pick up and k. 10 sts. up left back neck, 36 sts. down left front neck, and finally rib across 12 sts. of button band – 148 sts.
Work in double rib as set for bands for 1 row.
Now work the 2 buttonhole rows again.
Rib 6 more rows.
Cast off fairly loosely ribwise.

MAKING UP

With centre of cast-off edges of sleeves to shoulder seams, sew sleeves carefully into armholes easing to fit. Join side and sleeve seams. Stitch on front bands, stretching slightly to fit. Sew on buttons to correspond with buttonholes.

EMBROIDERY INSTRUCTIONS

Now work embroidery from appropriate chart on each front, in cross stitch, using a tapestry needle.

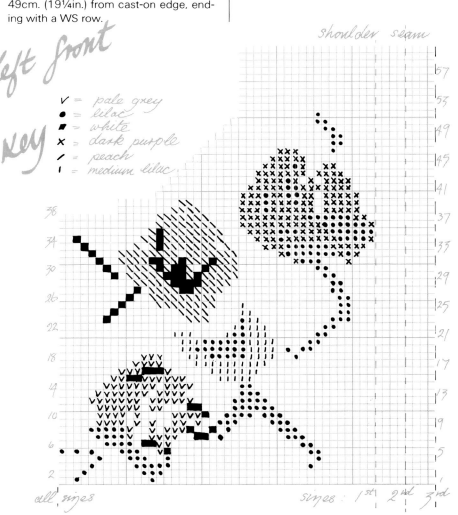

Left front

Key:
V = pale grey
● = lilac
■ = white
x = dark purple
/ = peach
| = medium lilac

shoulder seam

all sizes

sizes: 1st 2nd 3rd

DELICATES

CROSSOVER

ANGORA SWEATER WITH CROSSOVER FRONT

MATERIALS

13(14, 15) 20 g. balls Jaeger Angoraspun in pale green; a pair each 2¾mm. (no. 12), 3mm. (no. 11) and 3¼mm. (no. 10) knitting needles; stitch holder.

The quantities of yarn given are based on average requirements and are therefore approximate.

TENSION

25 sts. and 35 rows to 10cm. (4in.) on 3¼mm. needles over st.st.

MEASUREMENTS

To fit bust: 87(91, 97)cm. (34(36, 38)in.)

Actual measurement: 97(101, 107)cm. (38(40, 42)in.)

Length from centre back (including band): 58(59, 60)cm. (22¾(23¼, 23¾)in.)

Sleeve seam: 47(48, 49)cm. (18½(19, 19¼)in.)

Figures in brackets refer to the larger sizes. Where only one figure is given this refers to all sizes.

ABBREVIATIONS

k. knit; *p.* purl; *st(s).* stitch(es); *inc.* increase; *st.st.* stocking stitch; *foll.* following; *dec.* decrease; *rem.* remaining; *alt.* alternate; *beg.* beginning; *RS.* right side; *WS.* wrong side; *g.* grammes; *cm.* centimetres; *mm.* millimetres; *in.* inches; *rep.* repeat; *tog.* together; *cont.* continue.

BACK

With 3mm. needles, cast on 121(127, 133) sts., and work in single rib as follows:
Row 1 (RS): K.1, * p.1, k.1, rep. from * to end.
Row 2: P.1, * k.1, p.1, rep. from * to end.
Rep. last 2 rows until rib measures 20(20, 21)cm. (8(8, 8¼)in.) ending with a 2nd row.**
Change to 3¼mm. needles, and starting with a k. row work in st.st. until back measures 56(57, 58)cm. (22(22½, 23)in.) from cast-on edge, ending with a WS row.

SHAPE BACK NECK

Next row: K.24(27, 30), k.2 tog., turn, and work on this first set of sts. only.
*** Dec. 1 st. at neck edge on every row until 20(23, 26) sts. remain, thus ending at side edge.
Cast off sts. fairly loosely.
With RS facing return to rem. sts., cast off centre 69 sts. k.2 tog., then k. to end of row.
Work 1 row.
Now work as for first side from *** to end.

FRONT

Work as for back to **.
Change to 3¼mm. needles, and cont. as follows:
Next row (RS): Slip the first 39(42, 45)

sts. onto a stitch holder and work over the last set of 82(85, 88) sts. only.
Starting with a k. row work 10 rows in st.st.
**** Now dec. 1 st. at beg. (inside edge) on next row and then at this edge on every foll. alt. row until 20(23, 26) sts. remain. If necessary, work a few rows straight until front measures the same as back to shoulder cast-off edge, ending at side edge.
Cast off sts. fairly loosely.
Return to rem. 39(42, 45) sts., and with RS facing k. 1 row.
Next row: Cast on 43 sts., then p. these sts., and remainder of row 82(85, 88) sts. Work 9 more rows in st.st.
Now work as for first side from **** to end.

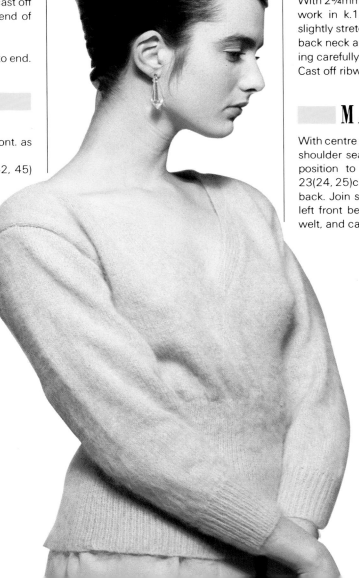

SLEEVES
(make 2)

With 2¾mm. needles, cast on 53(53, 59) sts., and work in single rib as for back welt for 9cm. (3½in.), ending with a 2nd row and working 15(17, 19) incs. evenly spaced along last row – 68(70, 78) sts.
Change to 3¼mm. needles, and starting with a k. row work in st.st., inc. 1 st. at each end of next row and then every foll. 6th row until there are 112(116, 122) sts. on the needle.
Now cont. straight until sleeve measures 47(48, 49)cm. (18½(19, 19¼)in.) from cast-on edge, ending with a WS row.
Cast off sts. fairly loosely.

FRONT BAND

Join both shoulder seams.
With 2¾mm. needles, cast on 12 sts., and work in k.1, p.1, rib, until band, when slightly stretched, fits up right front, along back neck and down left front neck, sewing carefully in position as you go along.
Cast off ribwise.

MAKING UP

With centre of cast-off edges of sleeves to shoulder seams, sew sleeves carefully in position to give an armhole depth of 23(24, 25)cm. (9(9½, 10)in.) on front and back. Join side and sleeve seams. Stitch left front behind right front along top of welt, and catch stitch bands at base.

64

RIBBONS

MOHAIR SWEATER WITH COLLAR CROCHETED WITH RIBBON YARN

MATERIALS

8 50 g. balls Pingouin Mohair 50 in pale pink; 3 50 g. balls Avocet Soiree in beige; a pair each 8mm. (no. 0) and 9mm. (no. 00) knitting needles; a crochet hook (optional).

The quantities of yarn given are based on average requirements and are therefore approximate.

TENSION

10 sts. and 13 rows to 10cm. (4in.) on 9mm. needles over pattern using mohair double.

MEASUREMENTS

To fit bust: 87–101cm. (34–40in.) – one size only.
Actual measurement: 136cm. (53½in.)
Length from shoulder: 64cm. (25¼in.)
Sleeve seam: 43cm. (17in.)

ABBREVIATIONS

k. knit; *p.* purl; *st(s).* stitch(es); *cm.* centimetres; *mm.* millimetres; *in.* inches; *g.* grammes; *alt.* alternate; *beg.* beginning; *cont.* continue; *dec.* decrease; *foll.* following; *inc.* increase; *patt.* pattern; *rem.* remaining; *rep.* repeat; *RS.* right side; *WS.* wrong side.

NOTE

Mohair is used *double* throughout. Soiree is used *single* throughout.

BACK

With 8mm. needles and mohair double, cast on 70 sts., and work in double rib as follows:

Row 1 (RS): K.2, * p.2, k.2, rep. from * to end.

Row 2: P.2, * k.2, p.2, rep. from * to end.

Rep. last 2 rows until 10 rows have been worked in all.

Change to 9mm. needles, and cont. in pattern as follows:

Row 1 (RS): P.10, * k.2, p.10, rep. from * to end.

Row 2: K.10, * p.2, k.10, rep. from * to end.

Rows 3-5: Rep. rows 1, 2 and 1.

Row 6: With soiree, work as row 2.

Row 7: With soiree, work as row 1.

Row 8: With mohair double, work as row 2.

Rows 9-12: With mohair double, rep. rows 1 and 2 twice.

These 12 rows form the patt. and are repeated throughout.

Cont. straight in patt. until back measures 64cm. (25¼in.) from cast-on edge, ending with a WS row.

SHAPE SHOULDERS

Keeping patt. correct, cast off 11 sts. at beg. of next 4 rows.

Cast off rem. 26 sts. fairly tightly.

FRONT

Work as for back until front measures 58cm. (23in.) from cast-on edge, ending with a WS row.

SHAPE FRONT NECK

Next row: Patt. 28, turn, and work on this first set of sts. only.

** Keeping patt. correct, dec. 1 st. at neck edge on every row until 22 sts. remain.

Now work a few rows straight until front measures the same as back to beg. of shoulder shaping, ending at side edge.

SHAPE SHOULDER

Keeping patt. correct, cast off 11 sts. at beg. of next row and foll. alt. row.

With RS facing rejoin yarn to rem. sts., cast off centre 14 sts., patt. to end.

Now work as for first side from ** to end.

SLEEVES
(make 2)

With 8mm. needles and mohair double, cast on 30 sts., and work in double rib as for back welt for 9 rows.

Increase row: Rib 4, (inc. in next st., rib 1) to last 4 sts., inc. in next st., rib 3 – 42 sts.

Change to 9mm. needles, and cont. in pattern as follows:

Row 1 (RS): P.8, * k.2, p.10, rep. from * to last 10 sts., k.2, p.8.

Cont. in patt. as now placed, working as for back, *at the same time*, inc. 1 st. at both ends of 9th row and then every foll. 8th row until there are 52 sts. on the needle, working inc. sts. into the patt. on either side.

Now work a few rows straight until sleeve measures 43cm. (17in.) from cast-on edge, ending with a WS row.

Cast off all sts. fairly tightly.

COLLAR

With 8mm. needles and mohair double, cast on 62 sts., and work in double rib as for back welt for 16 rows.

Cast off fairly loosely ribwise.

MAKING UP

Work vertical stripes in soiree between the 2 k. sts. of patt., either using a crochet hook or working in chain stitch with a darning needle. Join both shoulder seams. With a flat seam, join first 6 rows of collar, then sew collar to neck edge, placing seam at centre front. With centre of cast-off edges of sleeves to shoulder seams, sew sleeves in position reaching down to same depth on front and back. Join side and sleeve seams. If desired, tape shoulder seams to prevent garment stretching.

LACE

**COTTON DRESS TRIMMED WITH LACE,
WITH GARTER-STITCH STRAPS CROSSED AT THE BACK**

MATERIALS

5(6, 6) 50 g. balls Pingouin Coton Naturel 8 Fils in pale pink; *OR* 5(6, 6) 50 g. balls Pingouin Cotonnade in pale pink.
A pair each 3¾mm. (no. 9) and 4mm. (no. 8) knitting needles; 1 metre (1¼ yards) cotton lace edging.
The quantities of yarn given are based on average requirements and are therefore approximate.

TENSION

21 sts. and 24 rows to 10cm. (4in.) on 4mm. needles over st.st.

MEASUREMENTS

To fit chest/bust: 71(76, 81)cm. (28(30, 32)in.)
Length from cast-off edge of back to hem: 48(49, 50)cm. (19(19¼, 19¾)in.)
Figures in brackets refer to the larger sizes. Where only one figure is given this refers to all sizes.

ABBREVIATIONS

k. knit; *p.* purl; *st(s).* stitch(es); *RS.* right side; *WS.* wrong side; *skpo.* slip 1 st., k.1 st., pass slipped st. over; *cont.* continue; *rep.* repeat; *st.st.* stocking stitch; *cm.* centimetres; *mm.* millimetres; *in.* inches; *g.* grammes; *tog.* together; *g.st.* garter stitch; *rem.* remaining.

FRONT

Work as for back to **.
Starting with a k. row, work in st.st. until back measures 46(47, 48)cm. (18(18½, 19)in.) from cast-on edge, ending with a RS row.

SHAPE FRONT NECK AND SIDES

Row 1: K.9, p.18(20, 22), k.17, p.18(20, 22), k.9.
Row 2 (RS): K.
Rep. these 2 rows once more.
Next row (WS): Cast off 6 sts. k.wise, k.3, p.18(20, 22), k.3, cast off middle 11 sts. k.wise, k.3, p.18(20, 22), k.3, cast off 6 sts. k.wise.
With RS facing rejoin yarn, and cont. on this first set of sts. only.
Row 1: K.3, skpo., k. to last 5 sts., k.2 tog., k.3.
Row 2: K.3, p. to last 3 sts., k.3.
Rep. last 2 rows until 8 sts. remain.
Next row (WS): K.3, p.2 tog., k.3 – 7 sts.
Change to 3¾mm. needles.

WORK STRAPS

Work in g.st. (every row k.), cont. straight until strap measures 35(36, 37)cm. (13¾(14¼, 14½)in.).
Cast off.
With RS facing rejoin yarn to rem. sts. and work to match first side.

MAKING UP

Join side seams. Cross straps and stitch to back cast-off edge, 7cm. (2¾in.), in from each side seam.

LACE TRIMMING

Cut 1 metre (1¼ yards) of lace edging in half. Gather each piece into a frill and stitch to front of dress, beg. and ending at the bottom of each strap as shown in photo.

BACK

With 3¾mm. needles, cast on 71(75, 79) sts., and k.3 rows.
Change to 4mm. needles.**
Starting with a k. row, work in st.st. until back measures 46(47, 48)cm. (18(18½, 19)in.) from cast-on edge, ending with a WS row.
Change to 3¾mm. needles, and work in single rib as follows:
Row 1 (RS): K.1, * p.1, k.1, rep. from * to end.
Row 2: P.1, * k.1, p.1, rep. from * to end.
Rep. last 2 rows once more.
Cast off fairly loosely ribwise.

PEARL

**COTTON CARDIGAN WITH A CABLE,
TRIMMED WITH LACE**

MATERIALS

10(11, 11) 50 g. balls Pingouin Coton Naturel 8 Fils in pale pink; *OR* 10(11, 11) 50 g. balls Pingouin Cotonnade in pale pink.

A pair each 3¼mm. (no. 10) and 4mm. (no. 8) knitting needles; a cable needle; 4 pearl buttons; 2 metres (2½ yards) lace edging.

The quantities of yarn given are based on average requirements and are therefore approximate.

TENSION

21 sts. and 24 rows to 10cm. (4in.) on 4mm. needles over st.st.

MEASUREMENTS

To fit chest/bust: 71(76, 81)cm. (28(30, 32)in.)

Actual measurement: 91(95, 99)cm. (36(37½, 39)in.)

Length from shoulder: 46(48, 50)cm. (18(19, 19¾)in.)

Sleeve seam: 33(34, 35)cm. (13(13½, 13¾)in.)

Figures in brackets refer to the larger sizes. Where only one figure is given this refers to all sizes.

ABBREVIATIONS

k. knit; *p.* purl; *st(s).* stitch(es); *inc.* increase; *alt.* alternate; *C4F.* slip next 4 sts. onto cable needle and hold at front of work, k.4 then k.4 from cable needle; *patt.* pattern; *rep.* repeat; *st.st.* stocking stitch; *foll.* following; *cm.* centimetres; *mm.* millimetres; *in.* inches; *g.* grammes; *RS.* right side; *WS.* wrong side; *cont.* continue; *rem.* remaining; *dec.* decrease.

INSTRUCTIONS

BACK

With 3¼mm. needles, cast on 89(93, 97) sts., and work in single rib as follows:

Row 1 (RS): K.1, * p.1, k.1, rep. from * to end.

Row 2: P.1, * k.1, p.1, rep. from * to end.

Rep. last 2 rows until rib measures 4cm. (1½in.), ending with a 2nd row and working 10 incs. evenly spaced across last row – 99(103, 107) sts.

Change to 4mm. needles, and work in pattern as follows:

Row 1 (RS): K.25, p.2, k.8, p.2, k.25(29, 33), p.2, k.8, p.2, k.25.

Row 2: P.25, k.2, p.8, k.2, p.25(29, 33), k.2, p.8, k.2, p.25.

Rep. last 2 rows twice more.

Row 7: K.25, p.2, C4F., p.2, k.25(29, 33), p.2, C4F., p.2, k.25.

Row 8: As row 2.

Rows 9 and 10: As rows 1 and 2.

These 10 rows form the pattern and are repeated as required.

Cont. straight in patt. until back measures 44(46, 48)cm. (17¼(18, 18¾)in.) from cast-on edge, ending with a WS row.

SHAPE BACK NECK

Next row: Patt. 42(44, 46), cast off centre 15 sts., patt. to end of row and cont. on this last set of sts. only.

Patt. 1 row.

** Keeping patt. correct, cast off 6 sts. at neck edge on next row and foll. alt. row. Patt. 1 row, thus ending with a WS row. Cast off rem. 30(32, 34) sts.

With WS facing rejoin yarn to rem. sts. and work as for first side from ** to end, but patt. 2 rows before shoulder cast-off.

LEFT FRONT

With 3¼mm. needles, cast on 41(43, 45) sts., and work in single rib as for back welt for 4cm. (1½in.), ending with a 2nd row and working 6 incs. evenly spaced across last row – 47(49, 51) sts.

Change to 4mm. needles, and work in pattern as follows:

Row 1 (RS): K.25, p.2, k.8, p.2, k.10(12, 14).

The patt. is now placed. Cont. in patt. as set, working as for back, until front measures 25(27, 29)cm. (9¾(10¾, 11½)in.) from cast-on edge, ending with a WS row.

SHAPE FRONT NECK

Keeping patt. correct, dec. 1 st. at neck edge on next row and then every foll. 3rd row until 30(32, 34) sts. remain.

Now work a few rows straight until front measures the same as back to cast-off shoulder edge ending with a WS row.

Cast off all sts.

RIGHT FRONT

Work as for Left Front, but reversing all shapings, and position of cable panel.

SLEEVES
(make 2)

With 3¼mm. needles, cast on 41(43, 45) sts., and work in single rib as for back welt for 4cm. (1½in.) ending with a 2nd row and working 11 incs. evenly spaced across last row – 52(54, 56) sts.

Change to 4mm. needles, and starting with a k. row work in st.st., inc. 1 st. at each end of every foll. 4th row until there are 78(80, 82) sts. on the needle.

Now work straight until sleeve measures 33(34, 35)cm. (13(13½, 13¾)in.) from cast-on edge, ending with a WS row.

Cast off all sts.

FRONT BAND

Join both shoulder seams.

With 3¼mm. needles, cast on 10 sts.

Work in k.1, p.1, rib for 6 rows.

* *Buttonhole row (RS):* Rib 4, cast off 2 sts., rib to end.

Next row: Rib 4, cast on 2 sts., rib to end.

Work 18 rows in rib.

Cont. to rep. from * until the 4th buttonhole has been completed.

Now cont. straight in rib until band, when slightly stretched, fits up right front, around back neck and down left front, sewing in position as you go along.

Cast off ribwise.

MAKING UP

With centre of cast-off edges of sleeves to shoulder seams, sew sleeves carefully in position, reaching down to same depth on front and back. Join side and sleeve seams. Sew on buttons to correspond with buttonholes.

LACE TRIMMING

Cut the 2 metres (2½ yards) of lace edging in half. Gather each piece of lace and stitch to the outer edge of each front cable as shown in photo.

BABY SAILOR

CHILD'S SWEATER WITH CABLES AND A CENTRE FAIR ISLE PANEL

MATERIALS

9(10) 50 g. balls Pingouin Coton Naturel 8 Fils OR Pingouin Cotonnade in pale blue; 1 ball in cream; a pair each 3¼mm. (no. 10) and 4mm. (no. 8) knitting needles; a cable needle; 2 spare needles.

The quantities of yarn given are based on average requirements and are therefore approximate.

TENSION

21 sts. and 24 rows to 10cm. (4in.) on 4mm. needles over fair isle pattern.

MEASUREMENTS

To fit chest/bust: 66–71(76–81)cm. (26–28(30–32)in.)

Actual measurement: 85(100)cm. (33½ (39½)in.)

Length from shoulder: 43(47)cm. (17 (18½)in.)

Sleeve seam: 32(34)cm. (12½(13½)in.)

Figures in brackets refer to the larger size. Where only one figure is given this refers to both sizes.

ABBREVIATIONS

k. knit; *p.* purl; *st(s).* stitch(es); *inc.* increase; *dec.* decrease; *patt.* pattern; *foll.* following; *beg.* beginning; *rem.* remaining; *C4F.* slip next 4 sts. onto cable needle and hold at front of work, k.4 then k.4 from cable needle; *RS.* right side; *WS.* wrong side; *cm.* centimetres; *mm.* millimetres; *in.* inches; *g.* grammes; *rep.* repeat; *cont.* continue; *st.st.* stocking stitch; *tog.* together.

NOTE

When working from chart, read k. rows (odd numbered rows) from right to left and p. rows (even numbered rows) from left to right. Use separate balls of yarn for each area worked in cream, twisting yarns together on wrong side at joins to avoid making holes, and where convenient, strand yarn not in use loosely across wrong side of work, over not more than 3 sts. at a time to keep fabric elastic.

BACK

With 3¼mm. needles and pale blue, cast on 92(112) sts., and work in k.2, p.2, rib for 6cm. (2½in.), working 4 incs. evenly spaced across last row – 96(116) sts.

Change to 4mm. needles, and work in pattern and place chart as follows:

Row 1(RS): * P.2, k.8, rep. from * 2(3) times, p.2, k.1, now work across the 30 sts. of row 1 of chart, k.1, p.2, ** k.8, p.2, rep. from ** to end.

Row 2: * K.2, p.8, rep. from * 2(3) times, k.2, p.1, now work across the 30 sts. of row 2 of chart, p.1, k.2, ** p.8, k.2, rep. from ** to end.

Rep. last 2 rows twice more, but working rows 3, 4, 5 and 6 of chart.

Row 7: * P.2, C4F., rep. from * 2(3) times, p.2, k.1, now work across row 7 of chart, k.1, p.2, ** C4F., p. 2, rep. from ** to end.

Row 8: As row 2, but working row 8 of chart.

Row 9: As row 1, but working row 9 of chart.

Row 10: As row 2, but working row 10 of chart.

Rep. last 2 rows once more, but working

rows 11 and 12 of chart.

These 12 rows form the cable pattern for each side, and are repeated as required; over the centre 30 sts. work rows 1–70 of chart.

When chart is complete, cont. in st.st. in pale blue only, working cable patt. at each side as set until back measures 43(47)cm. (17(18½)in.) from cast-on edge, ending with a WS row.

SHAPE SHOULDERS

Keeping cable patt. correct, cast off 19(23) sts. at beg. of next 2 rows, and 13(19) sts. at beg. of foll. 2 rows.

Leave rem. 32 sts. on a spare needle.

FRONT

Work as for back until rows 1–70 of the chart have been completed.

Now cont. in st.st. in pale blue only, working cable patt. at each side as set for a further 0(10) rows.

SHAPE FRONT NECK

Next row (RS): Patt. 38(48), k.2 tog., turn, and work on this first set of sts. only.

*** Keeping cable patt. correct, dec. 1 st. at neck edge on every row until 32(42)sts. remain.

Now cont. straight until front measures the same as back to beg. of shoulder shaping, ending at side edge.

SHAPE SHOULDER

Keeping cable patt. correct, cast off 19(23) sts. at beg. of next row.

Work 1 row.

Cast off rem. 13(19) sts.

Return to rem. sts., and slip centre 16 sts. onto a spare needle, with RS facing rejoin yarn to rem. sts., k.2 tog., and patt. to end of row.

Now work as for first side from *** to end.

SLEEVES
(make 2)

With 3¼mm. needles and pale blue, cast on 44(48) sts., and work in k.2, p.2, rib for 5cm. (2in.), working 8(14) incs. evenly spaced across last row – 52(62) sts.

Change to 4mm. needles, and place cable patt. as for back, as follows:

Row 1 (RS): P.2, k.8, * rep. from * to last 2 sts., p.2.

Cont. in patt. as now set, *at the same time,* inc. 1 st. at each end of every foll. 5th row until there are 74(84) sts. on the needle, working inc. sts. into cable patt. on each side.

Now cont. straight until sleeve measures 32(34)cm. (12½(13½)in.) from cast-on edge, ending with a WS row.

Cast off all sts.

NECKBAND

Join right shoulder seam.

With 3¼mm. needles and pale blue and RS facing, pick up and k. 26 sts. down left front neck, k. across the 16 sts. at centre front, pick up and k. 26 sts. up right front neck and finally k. across the 32 sts. of back neck – 100 sts.

Work in k.2, p.2, rib for 7 rows.

Cast off ribwise.

MAKING UP

Join left shoulder and neckband seam. With centre of cast-off edges of sleeves to shoulder seams, sew sleeves carefully in position, reaching down to same depth on front and back. Join side and sleeve seams.

Press all seams.

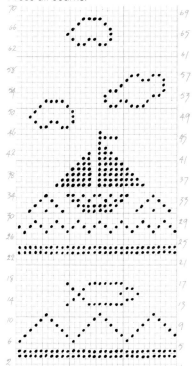

30 stitch pattern

Key □ = *pale blue*
• = *cream*

BRILLIANTS

OFF-THE-SHOULDER MOHAIR SWEATER PATTERNED IN ALLOVER ARAN TRELLIS

MATERIALS

7(8, 8) 50 g. balls Sirdar Nocturne in gala red, no. 530; a pair each 4½mm. (no. 7) and 5½mm. (no. 5) knitting needles; 4½mm. (no. 7) circular needle; a cable needle; 4 stitch holders.

The quantities of yarn given are based on average requirements and are therefore approximate.

TENSION

19½ sts. and 22½ rows to 10cm. (4in.) on 5½mm. needles over pattern.

MEASUREMENTS

To fit bust: 76–81(87–91, 97–101)cm. (30–32(34–36, 38–40)in.)

Actual measurement: 86(100, 114)cm. (34(39¼, 45)in.)

Length from back neck (excluding collar): 33(36, 39)cm. (13(14¼, 15¼)in.)

Sleeve seam: 36(38, 40)cm. (14¼(15, 15¾)in.)

Figures in brackets refer to the larger sizes. Where only one figure is given this refers to all sizes.

ABBREVIATIONS

k. knit; *p.* purl; *st(s).* stitch(es); *cm.* centimetres; *mm.* millimetres; *in.* inches; *g.* grammes; *RS.* right side; *WS.* wrong side; *tbl.* through back of loop; *rep.* repeat; *inc.* increase; *patt.* pattern; *dec.* decrease; *foll.* following; *C4F.* slip next 2 sts. onto cable needle and leave at front of work, k.2 then k.2 from cable needle; *FCr.* slip next 2 sts. onto cable needle and leave at front of work, k.1 then k.2 from cable needle; *BCr.* slip next st. onto cable needle and leave at back of work, k.2 then p. st. from cable needle; *FCP.* slip next 2 sts. onto cable needle and leave at front of work, p.1 then k.2 tbl. from cable needle; *alt.* alternate.

BACK & FRONT
(both alike)

With 4½mm. needles, cast on 77(87, 97) sts., and work in single rib as follows:

Row 1 (RS): K.1, * p.1, k.1. rep. from * to end.

Row 2: P.1, * k.1, p.1. rep. from * to end.

Rep. these 2 rows until rib measures 5cm. (2in.), ending with a 1st row.

Increase row: Rib 0(5, 3), [rib 5(3, 2), inc. in next st., rib 5(3, 3)] 7(11, 15) times, rib 0(5, 4) – 84(98, 112) sts.

Change to 5½mm. needles, and work in pattern as follows:

Row 1 (RS): * P.5, C4F., p.5, rep. from * to end.

Row 2: * K.5, p.4, k.5, rep. from * to end.

Row 3: * P.4, BCr., FCr., p.4, rep. from * to end.

Row 4: * K.4, p.3, k.1, p.2, k.4, rep. from * to end.

Row 5: * P.3, BCr., k.1, p.1, FCr., p.3, rep. from * to end.

Row 6: * K.3, p.3, k.1, p.1, k.1, p.2, k.3, rep. from * to end.

Row 7: * P.2, BCr., [k.1, p.1] twice, FCr., p.2, rep. from * to end.

Row 8: * K.2, p.3, [k.1, p.1] twice, k.1, p.2, k.2, rep. from * to end.

Row 9: * P.1, BCr., [k.1, p.1] 3 times, FCr., p.1, rep. from * to end.

Row 10: * K.1, p.3 [k.1, p.1] 3 times, k.1, p.2, k.1, rep. from * to end.

Row 11: * BCr., [k.1, p.1] 4 times, FCr., rep. from * to end.

Row 12: * P.3, [k.1, p.1] 4 times, k.1, p.2, rep. from * to end.

Row 13: K.2, [k.1, p.1] 5 times, * C4F., [k.1, p.1] 5 times, rep. from * to last 2 sts., k. 2.

Row 14: * P.2, [k.1, p.1] 5 times, p.2, rep. from * to end.

Row 15: * FCP., [k.1, p.1] 4 times, BCr., rep. from * to end.

Row 16: * K.1, p.2, [k.1, p.1] 4 times, p.2, k.1, rep. from * to end.

Row 17: * P.1, FCP., [k.1, p.1] 3 times, BCr., p.1, rep. from * to end.

Row 18: * K.2, p.2, [k.1, p.1] 3 times, p.2, k.2, rep. from * to end.

Row 19: * P.2, FCP., [k.1, p.1] twice, BCr., p.2, rep. from * to end.

Row 20: * K.3, p.2, [k.1, p.1] twice, p.2, k.3, rep. from * to end.

Row 21: * P.3, FCP., k.1, p.1, BCr., p.3, rep. from * to end.

Row 22: * K.4, p.2, k.1, p.3, k.4, rep. from * to end.

Row 23: * P.4, FCP., BCr., p.4, rep. from * to end.

Row 24: As row 2.

These 24 rows form the patt., and are repeated as required.

Work a further 6(8, 10) rows in patt. as set, thus ending with a WS row.

SHAPE RAGLAN ARMHOLES

Keeping patt. correct, dec. 1 st. at each end of next row and then every foll. 3rd row until 62(72, 82) sts. remain, ending with a WS row. Leave sts. on a stitch holder for collar.

SLEEVES
(make 2)

With 4½mm. needles, cast on 39(41, 43) sts., and work in single rib as given for back/front welt for 7cm. (2¾in.), ending with a 1st row.

Increase row: Rib 2(5, 2), [inc. in next st., rib 1(1, 2)] 17(15, 13) times, rib 3(6, 2) – 56 sts.

Change to 5½mm. needles, and work in patt. as given for back, *at the same time,* inc. 1 st. at each end of 19th(13th, 7th) row and then every foll. 4th row until there are 76(82, 86) sts. on the needle, working inc. sts. into patt. at either side.

Now cont. straight until sleeve measures 36(38, 40)cm. (14¼(15, 15¾)in.) from cast-on edge, ending with a WS row.

SHAPE RAGLAN TOP

Keeping patt. correct, dec. 1 st. at each end of next row and then every foll. alt. row until 50(50, 44) sts. remain, then 1 st. at each end of every row until 38(38, 40) sts. remain, ending with a WS row. Leave sts. on a stitch holder for collar.

COLLAR

Join raglan seams, leaving left back raglan open.

With the 4½mm. circular needle and RS facing, k. across 38(38, 40) sts. of left sleeve, 62(72, 82) sts. of front, 38(38, 40) sts. of right sleeve and 62(72, 82) sts. of back – 200(220, 244) sts.

Decrease row (WS): * P.3(4, 1), (p.2(3, 4), p.2 tog., p.3(3, 4)) 8 times, p.3(4, 1), now work across sleeve sts. as follows:

P.1(1, 2), (p.3(3, 2), p.2 tog., p.4(4, 2)) 4(4, 6) times, p.1(1, 2)*, now work from * to * once more – 176(196, 216) sts.

Work in rows of k.1, p.1, rib for 16cm. (6¼in.). Cast off loosely ribwise.

MAKING UP

Join left back raglan seam and collar, reversing seam on collar for turn down section. Join side and sleeve seams, using a fine back stitch.

INSTRUCTIONS

RHINESTONES

BAGGY MOHAIR SWEATER IN LACE, WITH V-NECK

MATERIALS

10(11) balls Sirdar Nocturne in fuchsia, no. 573; a pair each 5mm. (no. 6) and 5½mm. (no. 5) knitting needles; spare needle; safety pin.

The quantities of yarn given are based on average requirements and are therefore approximate.

TENSION

16 sts. and 16 rows to 10cm. (4in.) on 6mm. needles over pattern.

MEASUREMENTS

To fit bust: 87–91(91–97)cm. (34–36(36–38)in.)

Actual measurement: 125(133)cm. (49¼(52¼)in.)

Length from shoulder: 69(71)cm. (27(28)in.)

Sleeve seam: 46cm. (18in.)

Figures in brackets refer to the larger size. Where only one figure is given this refers to both sizes.

ABBREVIATIONS

k. knit; *p.* purl; *st(s).* stitch(es); *mm.* millimetres; *cm.* centimetres; *in.* inches; *g.* grammes; *RS.* right side; *WS.* wrong side; *rep.* repeat; *inc.* increase; *tog.* together; *yf.* yarn forward; *tbl.* through back of loop; *yrn.* yarn round needle; *sl.* slip; *psso.* pass slipped st. over; *cont.* continue; *patt.* pattern; *beg.* beginning; *foll.* following; *rem.* remaining; *dec.* decrease; *alt.* alternate.

BACK

With 5mm. needles, cast on 73(79) sts., and work in single rib as follows:

Row 1 (RS): K.1, * p.1, k.1, rep. from * to end.

Row 2: P.1, * k.1, p.1, rep. from * to end.

Rep. last 2 rows until rib measures 7cm. (2¾in.), ending with a 1st row.

Increase row: Rib 9(11), (inc. in next st., rib 1) 27(28) times, rib 10(12) – 100(107) sts.

Change to 5½mm. needles, and work in pattern as follows:

Row 1 (RS): K.1, * k.2, k.2 tog., yf., k.3, rep. from * to last st., k.1.

Row 2: P.1, * p.1, p.2 tog. tbl., yrn., p.1, yrn., p.2 tog., p.1, rep. from * to last st., p.1.

Row 3: K.1, * k.2 tog., yf., k.3, yf., sl.1, k.1, psso., rep. from * to last st., k.1.

Row 4: P.

Row 5: K.1, * yf., sl.1, k.1, psso., k.5, rep. from * to last st., k.1.

Row 6: P.1, * yrn., p.2 tog., p.2, p.2 tog. tbl., yrn., p.1, rep. from * to last st., p.1.

Row 7: K.1, * k.2, yf., sl.1, k.1, psso., k.2 tog., yf., k.1, rep. from * to last st., k.1.

Row 8: P.

These 8 rows form the pattern and are repeated throughout.

Cont. straight in patt. until back measures 69(71)cm. (27(28)in.) from cast-on edge, ending with a WS row.

SHAPE SHOULDERS

Keeping patt. correct, cast off 14 sts. at beg. of next 2 rows, and 16(18) sts. at beg. of foll. 2 rows.

Leave rem. 40(43) sts. on a spare needle.

FRONT

Work as given for back until front measures 38(40)cm. (15(15¾)in.) from cast-on edge, ending with a WS row.

SHAPE FRONT NECK

Next row: Patt. 47(51), k.2 tog., turn and work on this first set of sts. only.

** Keeping patt. correct, dec. 1 st. at neck edge on every foll. alt. row until 30(32) sts. remain.

Now work straight until front measures the same as back to beg. of shoulder shaping, ending at side edge.

SHAPE SHOULDER

Cast off 14 sts. at beg. of next row. Work 1 row. Cast off rem. 16(18) sts.

Return to rem. sts. and slip centre 2(1) st(s). onto a safety pin, with RS facing rejoin yarn to rem. sts. k.2 tog. and patt. to end of row.

Now work as for first side from ** to end.

SLEEVES

(make 2)

With 5mm. needles, cast on 41 sts., and work in single rib as given for back welt for 13 rows.

Increase row: Rib 4, (inc. in next st., rib 1) 17 times, rib 3 – 58 sts.

Change to 5½mm. needles, and work in patt. as given for back, *at the same time,* inc. 1 st. at each end of 13th row and then every foll. 4th row until there are 76 sts. on the needle, working inc. sts. into the patt. on either side.

Now cont. straight until sleeve measures 46cm. (18in.) from cast-on edge, ending with a WS row.

Cast off all sts. fairly loosely.

NECKBAND

Join right shoulder seam.

With 5mm. needles and RS facing, pick up and k. 50 sts. down left side of front neck, k. the 2(1) st(s). at centre front, pick up and k. 50 sts. up right side of front neck and finally k. across the 40(43) sts. at back neck – 142(144) sts.

Next row (WS): P.0(1), (k.1, p.1) 44(45) times, sl.1, k.1, psso., p. centre 2(1) st(s)., k.2 tog., (p.1, k.1) 24 times.

Next row: Work 47 sts. in rib as set, sl.1, k.1, psso., k. centre 2(1) st(s)., k.2 tog., rib to end.

Cont. in rib as set, dec. 1 st. in this way at each side of centre 2(1) st(s)., on every row until 15 rows in all have been worked. Cast off ribwise, dec. on this row as before.

MAKING UP

Join left shoulder and neckband seam. With centre of cast-off edges of sleeves to shoulder seams, sew sleeves carefully in position reaching down to same depth on front and back. Join side and sleeve seams.

ethnic FAIRISLE

PRINTOUT

FAIR ISLE COTTON SWEATER IN GEOMETRIC PATTERN

MATERIALS

11(12, 13) 50 g. balls Pingouin Coton
Naturel 8 Fils in cream; 6(7, 7) balls in
navy; a pair each 3¼mm. (no. 10) and
4mm. (no. 8) knitting needles; 2 spare
needles.
*The quantities of yarn given are based on
average requirements and are therefore
approximate.*

TENSION

21 sts. and 24 rows to 10cm. (4in.) on
4mm. needles over fair isle pattern.

MEASUREMENTS

To fit chest: 97(101, 107)cm. (38(40,
42)in.)
Actual measurement: 106(110, 116)cm.
(41¾(43¼, 45¾)in.)
Length from shoulder: 63(64, 65)cm.
(24¾(25¼, 25½)in.)
Sleeve seam: 51cm. (20in.)
*Figures in brackets refer to the larger
sizes. Where only one figure is given this
refers to all sizes.*

ABBREVIATIONS

k. knit; *p.* purl; *st(s).* stitch(es); *cm.* centimetres; *mm.* millimetres; *in.* inches; *g.*
grammes; *WS.* wrong side; *RS.* right side;
patt. pattern; *inc.* increase; *st.st.* stocking
stitch; *beg.* beginning; *foll.* following; *tog.*
together; *rem.* remaining; *dec.* decrease;
rep. repeat; *cont.* continue.

NOTE

When working from chart, read k. rows
(odd numbered rows) from right to left
and p. rows (even numbered rows) from
left to right. Strand yarn not in use loosely
across wrong side of work over not more
than 3 sts. at a time to keep fabric elastic.

INSTRUCTIONS

BACK

With 3¼mm. needles and cream, cast on 102(106, 110) sts., and work in double rib as follows:

Row 1 (RS): K.2, * p.2, k.2, rep. from * to end.

Row 2: P.2, * k.2, p.2, rep. from * to end.

Rep. last 2 rows until rib measures 8cm. (3in.), ending with a 2nd row and working 10(10, 12) incs. evenly spaced across last row – 112(116, 122) sts.

Change to 4mm. needles, and starting with a k. row work in st.st. as follows:

PLACE CHART

Row 1 (RS): Work 1(3, 1) st(s). before the dotted line, rep. the 10 st. patt. to last 1(3, 1) st(s)., work 1(3, 1) st(s). beyond the dotted line.

The chart is now set.

Cont. in patt. until the 46 rows of chart have been worked twice.

(92 patt. rows worked in all.)**

Now work rows 1–40(44, 46) once more, thus ending with a WS. row.

Now cont. in st.st. in cream only.

SHAPE SHOULDERS

Cast off 15 sts. at beg. of next 2 rows and 16(18, 21) sts. at beg. of foll. 2 rows.

Leave rem. 50 sts. on a spare needle.

FRONT

Work as for back to **.

Now work rows 1–24(28, 30) once more, thus ending with a WS row.

SHAPE FRONT NECK

Cont. in fair isle to match back and work as follows:

Next row: Patt. 43(45, 48) sts., k.2 tog., turn, and work on this first set of sts. only.

*** Keeping patt. correct, dec. 1 st. at neck edge on every row until 31(33, 36) sts. remain.

Now work a few rows straight until front measures the same as back to beg. of shoulder shaping, ending at side edge.

SHAPE SHOULDER

Cast off 15 sts. at beg. of next row. Work 1 row.

Cast off rem. 16(18, 21) sts.

Return to rem. sts. and slip centre 22 sts. onto a spare needle, with RS. facing rejoin yarn to rem. sts., k.2 tog., and patt. to end of row.

Now work as for first side from *** to end.

SLEEVES
(make 2)

With 3¼mm. needles and cream, cast on 46(46, 54) sts., and work in double rib as for back welt for 6cm. (2½in.) ending with a 2nd row and working 16(16, 18) incs. evenly spaced across last row – 62(62, 72) sts.

Change to 4mm. needles, and starting with a k. row, work in patt. from chart, reading chart as for *1st size on back*, **at the same time,** inc. 1 st. at each end of every foll. 4th row until there are 108(110, 112) sts. on the needle, working inc. sts. into the patt. on either side.

Now cont. straight until the 46 rows of chart have been worked twice, then work rows 1–14 once more.

Work 2 more rows in st.st. in cream.

Cast off in cream.

COLLAR

Join right shoulder seam.

With 3¼mm. needles and RS. facing and cream, pick up and k. 20 sts. evenly down left front neck, k. across the 22 sts. at centre front, pick up and k. 20 sts. up right front neck, then k. across the 50 sts. of back neck – 112 sts.

Starting with a 2nd row, work in double rib as for back welt for 7cm. (2¾in.).

Cast off ribwise.

MAKING UP

Join left shoulder and collar seam. With centre of cast-off edges of sleeves to shoulder seams, sew sleeve carefully in position reaching down to same depth on front and back. Join side and sleeve seams. Press all seams.

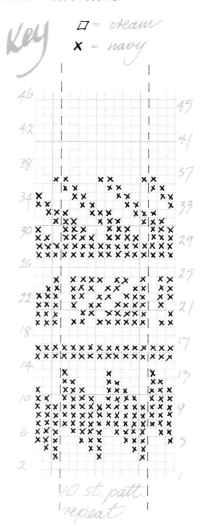

BIRDS

COTTON SWEATER WITH FAIR ISLE PATTERN
OF ETHNIC BIRDS

MATERIALS

16(17, 18) 50 g. balls Phildar Satine No. 5 in khaki; 3(3, 3) balls in cream; a pair each 3¼mm. (no. 10) and 4mm. (no. 8) knitting needles; a 3¼mm. (no. 10) circular needle; 1 spare needle; safety pin.
The quantities of yarn given are based on average requirements and are therefore approximate.

TENSION

22 sts. and 25 rows to 10cm. (4in.) on 4mm. needles over fair isle pattern.

MEASUREMENTS

To fit bust: 87(91, 97)cm. (34(36, 38)in.)
Actual measurement: 109(112, 116)cm. (43(44, 45¾)in.)
Length from shoulder: 65(66, 67)cm. (25½(26, 26½)in.)
Sleeve seam: 46cm. (18in.)
Figures in brackets refer to the larger sizes. Where only one figure is given this refers to all sizes.

ABBREVIATIONS

k. knit; *p.* purl; *st(s).* stitch(es); *inc.* increase; *st.st.* stocking stitch; *cont.* continue; *patt.* pattern; *dec.* decrease; *foll.* following; *cm.* centimetres; *mm.* millimetres; *in.* inches; *g.* grammes; *RS.* right side; *WS.* wrong side; *rep.* repeat; *rem.* remaining; *tog.* together; *alt.* alternate.

NOTE

When working from charts, read k. rows (odd numbered rows) from right to left and p. rows (even numbered rows) from left to right. Strand yarn not in use loosely across wrong side of work over not more than 3 sts. at a time to keep fabric elastic. When working bird motifs, use separate balls of yarn for each motif worked, twisting yarns together on wrong side at joins to avoid making holes.

BACK

With 3¼mm. needles and khaki, cast on 110(114, 118) sts., and work in double rib as follows:

Row 1 (RS): K.2, * p.2, k.2, rep. from * to end.

Row 2: P.2, * k.2, p.2, rep. from * to end.

Rep. last 2 rows until 22 rows in all have been worked, working 10 incs. evenly spaced across last row – 120(124, 128) sts.

Change to 4mm. needles, and starting with a k. row work 2 rows in st.st.

PLACE CHART A

Row 1 (RS): Work 0(2, 4) sts. before the dotted line, then rep. the 12 st. patt. to last 0(2, 4) sts., work 0(2, 4) sts. beyond the dotted line.

The chart is now placed.

Cont. as now set until the 20 rows of *Chart A* are complete.

Starting with a k. row work 4 rows in st.st. in khaki.

PLACE CHART B

Row 1 (RS): Work 0(2, 4) sts. in khaki, now rep. the 40 st. patt. 3 times, work 0(2, 4) sts. in khaki.

The charts are now placed.

Cont. as now set until the 20 rows of *Chart B* are complete.

Now cont. straight in st.st. in khaki only until back measures 64(65, 66)cm. (25¼(25½, 26)in.) from cast-on edge, ending with a WS row.

SHAPE BACK NECK

Next row: K.34(36, 38), k.2 tog., turn, and work on this first set of sts. only.

** Dec. 1 st. at neck edge on next 3 rows, thus ending at side edge.

Cast off rem. 32(34, 36) sts. fairly loosely.

Return to rem. sts. and slip centre 48 sts.

onto a spare needle, with RS. facing rejoin yarn to rem. sts., k.2 tog. and k. to end of row.

Work 1 row.

Now work as for first side from ** to end.

FRONT

Work as for back until front measures 36(37, 38)cm. (14¼(14½, 15)in.) from cast-on edge, ending with a WS row.

SHAPE V NECK

Next row: K.57(59, 61), k.2 tog., turn, and work on this first set of sts. only.

*** Dec. 1 st. at neck edge on every foll. alt. row until 48(50, 52) sts. remain.

Now dec. 1 st. at neck edge on every foll. 3rd row until 32(34, 36) sts. remain.

Now work a few rows straight until front measures the same as back to cast-off shoulder edge, ending at side edge.

Cast off sts. fairly loosely.

Return to rem. sts., and slip next 2 sts. onto a safety pin, k.2 tog., and k. to end of row.

Now work as for first side from *** to end.

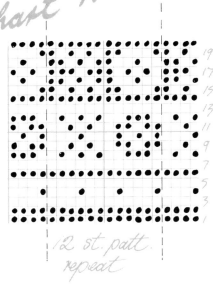

Chart A

12 st. patt. repeat

Chart B

40 st. patt.

Key

◻ = *khaki*

● = *cream*

SLEEVES

(make 2)

With 3¼mm. needles and khaki, cast on 46(46, 54) sts., and work in double rib as for back welt for 7cm. (2¾in.), ending with a 2nd row and working 26(26, 28) incs. evenly spaced across last row – 72(72, 82) sts.

Change to 4mm. needles, and starting with a k. row work in st.st., inc. 1 st. at each end of every foll. 4th row until there are 98(98, 108) sts. on the needle, ending with a WS row.

PLACE CHART A

Row 1(RS): Work 1(1, 0) st. before the dotted line, then rep. the 12 st. patt. to last 1(1, 0) st., work 1(1, 0) st. beyond the dotted line.

The chart is now placed.

Cont. to work from chart as set, *at the same time,* cont. to inc. 1 st. at each end of every foll. 4th row as set, working inc. sts. into chart on either side, until there are 112(112, 122) sts. on the needle, and the 20 rows of *Chart A* have been worked twice.

Now cont. in khaki only for 4 rows.

Cast off all sts. fairly loosely.

NECKBAND

Join right shoulder seam.

With the 3¼mm. circular needle and khaki and RS facing, pick up and k. 70 sts. down left front neck, k. across the 2 sts. on safety pin, pick up and k. 70 sts. up right front neck, 6 sts. down right back neck, k. across the 48 sts. at back neck and finally pick up and k. 6 sts. up left back neck – 202 sts.

Work in k.2, p.2, rib, dec. 1 st. at each side of 2 centre front sts. on every row.

Cont. as set until 15 rib rows have been worked.

Cast off ribwise, dec. 1 st. at each side of centre 2 sts. as before.

MAKING UP

Join left shoulder and neckband seam. With centre of cast-off edges of sleeves to shoulder seams, sew sleeves carefully in position reaching down to same depth on front and back. Join side and sleeve seams. Press all seams.

WILD HORSES

COTTON SWEATER AND SKIRT, PATTERNED WITH A HORSE MOTIF

MATERIALS

SWEATER:

15(16) 50 g. balls Rowan Handknit D.K. Cotton in cream; 3(3) balls in black; 2 spare needles.

SKIRT:

5(6) 50 g. balls Rowan Handknit D.K. Cotton in cream; 2(2) balls in black; waist length elastic (optional).

FOR BOTH:

A pair each 3¾mm. (no. 9) and 4mm. (no. 8) knitting needles.
The quantities of yarn given are based on average requirements and are therefore approximate.

TENSION

21 sts. and 25 rows to 10cm. (4in.) on 4mm. needles over st.st.

MEASUREMENTS

To fit bust: 87–91(91–97)cm. (34–36(36–38)in.)
Actual sweater measurement: 114(121)cm. (45(47¾)in.)
Length from shoulder: 65(67)cm. (25½(26½)in.)
Sleeve seam: 47(48)cm. (18½(19)in.)
To fit hips: 87–91(91–97)cm. (34–36(36–38)in.)
Total length of skirt (waist rib unfolded): 53(55)cm. (21(21¾)in.)
Figures in brackets refer to the larger size. Where only one figure is given this refers to both sizes.

ABBREVIATIONS

k. knit; *p.* purl; *st(s).* stitch(es); *inc.* increase; *st.st.* stocking stitch; *patt.* pattern; *beg.* beginning; *RS.* right side; *WS.* wrong side; *foll.* following; *cm.* centimetres; *mm.* millimetres; *in.* inches; *g.* grammes; *D.K.* double knitting; *rep.* repeat; *cont.* continue; *rem.* remaining; *dec.* decrease; *alt.* alternate.

NOTE

When working in colour pattern from charts, strand yarn not in use loosely across wrong side of work over not more than 3 sts. at a time to keep fabric elastic. When working larger motifs of one colour, use separate balls of yarn for each colour area worked, twisting yarns together on wrong side at joins to avoid making holes. When reading charts, work k. rows (odd numbered rows) from right to left and p. rows (even numbered rows) from left to right.

SWEATER

BACK

With 3¾mm. needles and cream, cast on 118(126) sts., and work in double rib as follows:

Row 1 (RS): K.2, * p.2, k.2, rep. from * to end.

Row 2: P.2, * k.2, p.2, rep. from * to end.
Rep. last 2 rows until 16 rib rows in all have been worked, and inc. 2 sts. evenly across last row – 120(128) sts.
Change to 4mm. needles, and starting with a k. row work 2 rows in st.st.

PLACE CHART A

Next row (RS): Starting on Row 11, rep. the 4 st. patt. of *Chart A* 30(32) times across row.
Cont. to follow chart as now set, until Row 22 has been completed. Now cont. in st.st. in cream only until back measures 46(48)cm. (18(19)in.) from cast-on edge, ending with a WS row.

PLACE CHART B

Row 1 (RS): K.7(9) in cream, now work across the 30 sts. of Row 1 of *Chart B*, * k.8(10) in cream, now work across the 30 sts. of Row 1 of *Chart B* *, rep. from * to * once more, k.7(9) in cream.
Cont. as now set until the 22 rows of *Chart B* have been completed.
Work 2 rows in st.st. in cream.
Now starting with Row 1, work in patt. from *Chart A,* repeating the 4 st. patt. 30(32) times across row.
Cont. as now set until the 24 rows of *Chart A* have been completed, thus ending with a WS row.

SHAPE SHOULDERS

Work in cream only, cast off 18(20) sts. at beg. of next 2 rows, and 19(21) sts. at beg. of foll. 2 rows.
Leave rem. 46 sts. on a spare needle.

FRONT

Work as for back until the 22 rows of *Chart B* have been completed.
Work 2 rows in st.st. in cream.
Now work in patt. from *Chart A,* for 4 rows, thus ending with a WS row.

SHAPE FRONT NECK

Next row: (Row 5 of *Chart A*). Patt. 48(52), turn, and work on this first set of sts. only.
** Keeping chart correct, dec. 1 st. at neck edge on every row until 37(41) sts. remain.
Now cont. straight until front measures the same as back to beg. of shoulder shaping, ending at side edge (*Chart A*) is complete.

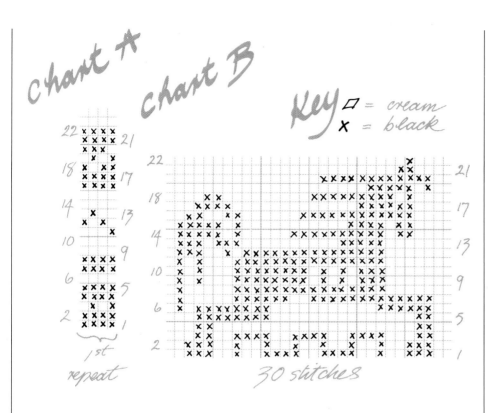

Chart A   Chart B

Key ⬜ = cream
    X = black

30 stitches

1st repeat

SHAPE SHOULDER

Work in cream only, cast off 18(20) sts. at beg. of next row and 19(21) sts. at beg. of foll. alt. row.
Return to rem. sts. and slip centre 24 sts. onto a spare needle, with RS. facing rejoin yarn to rem. sts. and patt. to end of row.
Now work as for first side from ** to end.

SLEEVES
(make 2)

With 3¾mm. needles and cream, cast on 62(66) sts., and work in double rib as for back welt for 19 rows, working 14 incs. evenly spaced across last row – 76(80) sts.
Change to 4mm. needles, and starting with a k. row work in st.st. as follows:

PLACE CHART A

Next row (RS): Starting on Row 11, rep. the 4 st. patt. of *Chart A* 19(20) times across row.
Cont. to follow chart as now set, *at the same time,* inc. 1 st. at each end of every foll. 6th row until there are 106(110) sts. on the needle, working inc. sts. into the patt. on either side. When the 12 rows of *Chart A* have been completed cont. in cream only, until 78(82) rows in all have been worked from top of rib.
Now starting with Row 1, work from *Chart A,* and when all incs. have been completed cont. straight until the 24 rows of chart are complete.
Cast off fairly loosely using cream.

NECKBAND

Join right shoulder seam.
With 3¾mm. needles and RS facing and cream, pick up and k. 20 sts. down left front neck, k. across the 24 sts. at centre front, pick up and k. 20 sts. up right front neck, then k. across the 46 sts. of back neck – 110 sts.
Starting with a 2nd row work in double rib as for back welt for 7 rows.
Cast off fairly loosely ribwise.

MAKING UP

Join left shoulder seam and neckband. With centre of cast-off edges of sleeves to shoulder seams, sew sleeves carefully in position reaching down to same depth on front and back. Join side and sleeve seams. Press all seams.

BACK & FRONT
(both alike)

With 3¾mm. needles and cream, cast on 96(104) sts., and work in k.1, p.1, rib for 7 rows, working an inc. at each end of last row worked – 98(106) sts.
Now starting with a k. row, work 2 rows in st.st., and inc. 1 st. at each end of last of these rows – 100(108) sts.
Change to 4mm. needles, and starting with a k. row work in st.st. as follows:

PLACE CHART A

Next row: Starting on Row 1, rep. the 4 st. patt. of *Chart A* 25(27) times across row. Cont. to follow chart as now set until the 24 rows have been completed, working an inc. at each end of last row – 102(110) sts.

PLACE CHART B

Row 1 (RS): K.2(4) in cream, now work across the 30 sts. of Row 1 of *Chart B, * k.4(6) in cream, now work across the 30 sts. of Row 1 of *Chart B *, rep. from * to * once more, k.2(4) in cream.
Cont. as now set until the 22 rows of *Chart B* have been completed.
Now cont. straight in cream only until skirt measures 30(32)cm. (11¾(12½)in.) from cast-on edge.
Now dec. 1 st. at each end of next row and every foll. 4th row until 86(94) sts. remain.
Cont. straight until skirt measures 44(46)cm. (17¼(18)in.) from cast-on edge, ending with a WS row.
Change to 3¾mm. needles, and work in k.1, p.1, rib for 9cm. (3½in.).
Cast off fairly loosely ribwise.

MAKING UP

Join side seams. Waistband can be left and belted unfolded for a longer length, or it can be folded in half to inside and stitched in position enclosing a waist length piece of elastic. Press seams.

ANCHOR

CHUNKY SWEATER WITH COLLAR, STRIPED SLEEVES AND ANCHOR MOTIF

MATERIALS

11(12, 13) 50 g. balls Patons Beehive Shetland Chunky in white; 2(3, 3) balls in navy; a pair each 4½mm. (no. 7) and 5½mm. (no. 5) knitting needles; a 4½mm. (no. 7) circular needle; 2 spare needles; crochet hook (optional).

The quantities of yarn given are based on average requirements and are therefore approximate.

TENSION

17 sts. and 20 rows to 10cm. (4in.) on 5½mm. needles over st.st.

MEASUREMENTS

To fit bust: 87(91, 97)cm. (34(36, 38)in.)
Actual measurement: 108(112, 117)cm. (42½(44, 46)in.)
Length from shoulder: 68(69, 70)cm. (26¾(27¼, 27½)in.)
Sleeve seam: 46cm. (18in.)

Figures in brackets refer to the larger sizes. Where only one figure is given this refers to all sizes.

ABBREVIATIONS

k. knit; **p.** purl; **st(s).** stitch(es); **inc.** increase; **dec.** decrease; **st.st.** stocking stitch; **beg.** beginning; **rem.** remaining; **tog.** together; **foll.** following; **cm.** centimetres; **mm.** millimetres; **in.** inches; **g.** grammes; **RS.** right side; **WS.** wrong side; **rep.** repeat; **cont.** continue.

NOTE

When working motif, do not strand yarn across wrong side of work, but twist yarns together on wrong side at joins to avoid making a hole. When reading chart, work k. rows (odd numbered rows) from right to left and p. rows (even numbered rows) from left to right.

BACK

With 4½mm. needles and white, cast on 91(95, 99) sts., and work in single rib as follows:

Row 1 (RS): K.1, * p.1, k.1, rep. from * to end.
Row 2: P.1, * k.1, p.1, rep. from * to end.
Rep. last 2 rows until rib measures 7cm. (2¾in.), ending with a 2nd row and working 1 inc. at end of last row – 92(96, 100) sts. **

Change to 5½mm. needles, and starting with a k. row, work in st.st. until back measures 68(69, 70)cm. (26¾(27¼, 27½)in.) from cast-on edge, ending with a WS row.

SHAPE SHOULDERS

Cast off 15(16, 17) sts. at beg. of next 4 rows.
Leave rem. 32 sts. on a spare needle.

FRONT

Work as for back to **.
Change to 5½mm. needles, and starting with a k. row, work 4 rows in st.st.

PLACE CHART

Row 1 (RS): K.14, now work across the 15 sts. of row 1 of chart, k. to end of row. The chart is now placed. Cont. to follow chart until the 21 rows are complete. Now cont. in white only.
Cont. straight until front measures 62(63, 64)cm. (24¼(24¾, 25)in.) from cast-on edge ending with a WS row.

SHAPE FRONT NECK

Next row: K.36(38, 40) sts., k.2 tog., turn, and work on this first set of sts. only.
*** *Next row:* Cast off 3 sts. (neck edge), work to end.
Now dec. 1 st. at neck edge on every row until 30(32, 34) sts. remain.
Work straight in st.st. until front measures same as back to beg. of shoulder shaping, ending at side edge.

SHAPE SHOULDER

Cast off 15(16, 17) sts. at beg. of next row.
Work 1 row, then cast off rem. 15(16, 17) sts.
Return to rem. sts. and slip centre 16 sts. onto a spare needle, with RS facing, rejoin yarn to rem. sts. k.2 tog. and work to end of row. Work 1 row.
Now work as for first side from *** to end.

SLEEVES
(make 2)

With 4½mm. needles and white, cast on 37(37, 41) sts. and work in single rib as for back welt for 18 rows, working 19 incs. evenly spaced across last row – 56(56, 60) sts.
Change to 5½mm. needles and starting with a k. row, work in st.st. for 4 rows.
Change to navy and work in st.st. for 16 rows, *at the same time* inc. 1 st. at each end of 1st, 6th and then every foll. 6th row. When the 16 rows of st.st. in navy have been completed change to white and work a stripe of 16 rows, continuing to inc. on every 6th row as set.
Keeping continuity of stripes, cont. as set until there are 84(84, 88) sts. on the needle. When the 3rd navy stripe has been completed, cast off in navy.
Join shoulder seams.

COLLAR

With the 4½mm. circular needle and white, work across the 32 sts. of back neck in k.1, p.1, rib, pick up and knit 14 sts. down left front neck, work over the 16 sts. of front neck in k.1, p.1, rib (marking the centre 2 sts. of front neck with a coloured thread), then pick up and knit 14 sts. up right front neck – 76 sts.
Work in *rounds* of k.1, p.1, rib until the 10th round has been completed, ending with one of the marked sts.
Divide collar: Rib back 1 row ending with 2nd marked st. Turn. Keep working in rib in rows, turning at each marked st. until 20 more rows have been completed.
Change to navy and work 2 rows in rib, then cast off ribwise in navy.
With a crochet hook, or by picking up and casting off with a knitting needle, work in navy along the 2 inside edges of collar. Fasten off.

MAKING UP

With centre of cast-off edges of sleeves to shoulder seams, sew sleeves carefully in position, reaching down to same depth on front and back. Join side and sleeve seams. Press all seams.

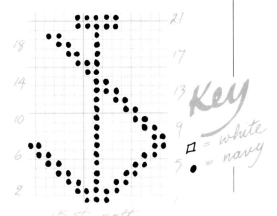

Key
☐ = white
● = navy

15 st. patt.

easy

CREAM

BARK

SHAGGY DOG

BONE

BARK

LABURNUM STITCH TUNIC WITH A DROPPED SHOULDER LINE AND COLLAR

MATERIALS

18(19, 20) 50 g. balls Patons Beehive Shetland Chunky in cream; a pair each 4½mm. (no. 7) and 5½mm. (no. 5) knitting needles; 2 spare needles.
The quantities of yarn given are based on average requirements and are therefore approximate.

TENSION

18 sts. and 21 rows to 10cm. (4in.) on 5½mm. needles over pattern.

MEASUREMENTS

To fit bust: 87(91, 97)cm. (34(36, 38)in.)
Actual measurement: 118(124, 130)cm. (46½(48¾, 51¼)in.)
Length from shoulder: 64(65, 66)cm. (25¼(25½, 26)in.)
Sleeve seam: 49cm. (19¼in.)
Figures in brackets refer to the larger sizes. Where only one figure is given this refers to all sizes.

ABBREVIATIONS

k. knit; *p.* purl; *st(s).* stitch(es); *inc.* increase; *rep.* repeat; *sl.* slip; *psso.* pass the slip stitch over; *tog.* together; *cont.* continue; *patt.* pattern; *foll.* following; *rem.* remaining; *yrn.* yarn round needle; *alt.* alternate; *cm.* centimetres; *mm.* millimetres; *in.* inches; *g.* grammes; *RS.* right side; *WS.* wrong side; *beg.* beginning; *dec.* decrease.

INSTRUCTIONS

NOTE

When working Row 3 of pattern, please note that stitch count varies. Take this into account when counting sts. when working shapings.

BACK

With 4½mm. needles, cast on 91(95, 99) sts., and work in single rib as follows:
Row 1 (RS): K.1, * p.1, k.1, rep. from * to end.
Row 2: P.1, * k.1, p.1, rep. from * to end.
Rep. last 2 rows until rib measures 7cm. (2¾in.), ending with a 2nd row and working 16(17, 18) incs. evenly spaced across last row – 107(112, 117) sts.
Change to 5½mm. needles, and work in pattern as follows:
Row 1 (RS): P.2, * k.3, p.2, rep. from * to end.
Row 2: K.2, * p.3, k.2, rep. from * to end.
Row 3: P.2, * sl. 1, k.2, psso, p.2, rep. from * to end.
Row 4: K.2, * p.1, yrn., p.1, k.2, rep. from * to end.
These 4 rows form the pattern and are repeated throughout.
Cont. straight in patt. until back measures 64(65, 66)cm. (25¼(25½, 26)in.) from cast-on edge, ending with a WS row.

SHAPE SHOULDERS

Keeping patt. correct, cast off 15(16, 17) sts. at beg. of next 4 rows.
Leave rem. 47(48, 49) sts. on a spare needle.

FRONT

Work as for back until front measures 58(59, 60)cm. (23(23¼, 23¾)in.) from cast-on edge, ending with a WS row.

SHAPE FRONT NECK

Next row: Patt. 40(42, 44), k.2 tog., turn, and work on this first set of sts. only.
** Keeping patt. correct, dec. 1 st. at neck edge on every row until 30(32, 34) sts. remain.
Now work a few rows straight until front measures the same as back to beg. of shoulder shaping, ending at side edge.

SHAPE SHOULDER

Keeping patt. correct, cast off 15(16, 17) sts. at beg. of next row and foll. alt. row.
Return to rem. sts., and slip centre 23(24, 25) sts. onto a spare needle.
With RS facing rejoin yarn to rem. sts., k.2 tog., and patt. to end of row.
Patt. 1 row.
Now work as for first side from ** to end.

SLEEVES
(make 2)

With 4½mm. needles, cast on 43(43, 47) sts., and work in single rib as for back welt for 7cm. (2¾in.), ending with a 2nd row and working 24(24, 25) incs. evenly spaced across last row – 67(67, 72) sts.
Change to 5½mm. needles, and work in patt. as for back, *at the same time*, inc. 1 st. at each end of next row and then every foll. 6th row until there are 97(97, 102) sts. on the needle, working inc. sts. into the patt. on either side.
Now work a few rows straight until sleeve measures 49cm. (19¼in.) from cast-on edge, ending with a WS. row.
Cast off all sts. fairly loosely.

COLLAR

Join right shoulder seam.
With 4½mm. needles and RS facing, pick up and k. 20 sts. down left front neck, work in k.1, p.1, rib across the 23(24, 25) sts. at centre front and working an inc. *for 1st size* and a dec. *for 3rd size* (24 sts. all sizes), then pick up and k. 20 sts. up right front neck, then work in k.1, p.1, rib across the 47(48, 49) sts. at back neck, working an inc. *for 1st size* and a dec. *for 3rd size* (48 sts. all sizes) – 112 sts.
Work in k.1, p.1, rib for 24cm. (9½in.).
Cast off fairly loosely ribwise.

MAKING UP

Join left shoulder seam and collar seam, reversing seam on collar for turn back section. With centre of cast-off edges of sleeves to shoulder seams, sew sleeves carefully in position, reaching down to same depth on front and back. Join side and sleeve seams. Press all seams.

SHAGGY DOG

CHUNKY CARDIGAN WITH CABLES
AND POCKET SET INTO THE SEAMS

MATERIALS

22(23, 24) 50 g. balls Pingouin Iceberg in cream; *OR* 15(16, 17) 50 g. balls Pingouin Confortable Sport in cream; a pair each 5mm. (no. 6) and 6mm. (no. 4) knitting needles; a cable needle; 7 buttons; spare needle; 2 safety pins.

The quantities of yarn given are based on average requirements and are therefore approximate.

TENSION

12 sts. and 16 rows to 10cm. (4in.) on 6mm. needles over st.st.

MEASUREMENTS

To fit bust: 87(91, 97)cm. (34(36, 38)in.)
Actual measurement: 130(135, 140)cm. (51(53, 55)in.)
Length from shoulder: 71(72, 73)cm. (28(28¼, 28¾)in.)
Sleeve seam: 48cm. (19in.)

Figures in brackets refer to the larger sizes. Where only one figure is given this refers to all sizes.

ABBREVIATIONS

k. knit; *p.* purl; *st(s).* stitch(es); *inc.* increase; *foll.* following; *beg.* beginning; *patt.* pattern; *cont.* continue; *C4F.* slip next 4 sts. onto a cable needle and hold at front of work, k.4 then k.4 sts. from cable needle; *rep.* repeat; *RS.* right side; *WS.* wrong side; *cm.* centimetres; *mm.* millimetres; *in.* inches; *g.* grammes; *st.st.* stocking stitch; *tog.* together; *dec.* decrease; *rem.* remaining.

BACK

With 5mm. needles, cast on 71(73, 75) sts., and work in single rib as follows:
Row 1 (RS): K.1, * p.1, k.1, rep. from * to end.
Row 2: P.1, * k.1, p.1, rep. from * to end.
Rep. last 2 rows until rib measures 6cm. (2½in.), ending with a 2nd row, and working 11 incs. evenly spaced across last row – 82(84, 86) sts.
Change to 6mm. needles and work in pattern as follows:
Row 1 (RS): K.14(15, 16), p.2, k.8, p.2, k.30, p.2, k.8, p.2, k.14(15, 16).
Row 2: P.14(15, 16), k.2, p.8, k.2, p.30, k.2, p.8, k.2, p.14(15, 16).
Rep. last 2 rows once more.
Row 5: K.14(15, 16), p.2, C4F., p.2, k.30, p.2, C4F., p.2, k.14(15, 16).
Row 6: As row 2.
Rows 7-10: Rep. rows 1 and 2 twice.
These 10 rows form the pattern and are repeated as required.
Cont. straight in patt. until back measures 69(70, 71)cm. (27(27½, 28)in.) from cast-on edge, ending with a WS row, placing coloured markers at each end of rows 16 and 35 to indicate pocket placement.

SHAPE BACK NECK

Next row: K.29(30, 31), k.2 tog., turn, and work on this first set of sts. only.
** Keeping patt. correct, dec. 1 st. at neck edge on the foll. row.
Work 2 rows straight, thus ending with a WS row.
Cast off rem. 29(30, 31) sts.
Return to rem. sts. and slip centre 20 sts. onto a spare needle.
With RS facing rejoin yarn to rem. sts., k.2 tog., and patt. to end of row.
Now work as for first side from ** to end.

RIGHT FRONT

With 5mm. needles, cast on 33(35, 37) sts., and work in single rib as for back welt for 6cm. (2½in.), ending with a 2nd row, and working 7 incs. evenly spaced across last row – 40(42, 44) sts.
Change to 6mm. needles and work in pattern as follows:
Row 1 (RS): K.14(15, 16), p.2, k.8, p.2, k.14(15, 16).
The patt. is now placed. Cont. in patt. as

now set, working as for back, until front measures 63(64, 65)cm. (24¾(25¼, 25¾)in.) from cast-on edge, ending at centre front edge, and placing coloured markers at side edge on rows 16 and 35 to indicate pocket placement.

SHAPE FRONT NECK

Keeping patt. correct, cast off 5 sts. at beg. (neck edge) on next row.
Now dec. 1 st. at neck edge on every row until 29(30, 31) sts. remain.
Now cont. straight until front measures the same as back to shoulder cast-off edge, ending with a WS row.
Cast off.

LEFT FRONT

Work as for Right Front, reversing all shapings.

SLEEVES
(make 2)

With 5mm. needles, cast on 29(31, 33) sts., and work in single rib as for back welt for 7cm. (2¾in.), ending with a 2nd row, and working 7 incs. evenly spaced across last row – 36(38, 40)sts.
Change to 6mm. needles, and starting with a k. row work in st.st., inc. 1 st. at each end of every foll. 4th row until there are 66(68, 70) sts. on the needle.
Now work straight until sleeve measures 48cm. (19in.) from cast-on edge, ending with a WS row.
Cast off all sts. fairly loosely.

FRONT BAND

With 5mm. needles, cast on 10 sts., and work in k1, p.1, rib for 6 rows.
* *Buttonhole row (RS):* Rib 4, cast off 2 sts., rib 4.
Next row: Rib 4, cast on 2 sts., rib 4.
Rib 16 rows.
Cont. to rep. from * until 6 buttonholes have been completed.
Rib 14(16, 18) rows, sewing band in position, slightly stretched, along right front edge as you go along.
Leave sts. on a safety pin.
Work another band for left front edge to match, but without buttonholes.

NECKBAND

Join both shoulder seams.
With 5mm. needles, and RS facing, rib across the 10 sts. of buttonhole band, then pick up and k. 20 sts. up right front neck, 6 sts. down right back neck, work in k.1, p.1, rib across the centre 20 sts. of back neck, then pick up and k. 6 sts. up left back neck, 20 sts. down left front neck and finally rib across the 10 sts. of button band – 92 sts.
Work in k.1, p.1, rib for 1 row.
Work the 2 buttonhole rows again.
Rib 4 more rows.
Cast off fairly loosely ribwise.

POCKET LININGS
(make 2)

With 6mm. needles, cast on 18 sts.
Starting with a k. row, work in st.st. for 44 rows.
Cast off fairly loosely.

MAKING UP

With centre of cast-off edges of sleeves to shoulder seams, sew sleeves carefully in position, reaching down to same depth on front and back. Join side and sleeve seams leaving seam between coloured markers on each side edge free. Sew on buttons to correspond with buttonholes. Fold each pocket lining in half and sew the cast-off and cast-on edges to the gap in the side seams, with the seams on the inside. Now stitch the sides of each pocket lining together.

BONE

CHUNKY SWEATER KNITTED IN RIDGES, WITH COLLAR

MATERIALS

13(14, 15) 50 g. balls Emu Superwash Chunky in cream; a pair each 4½mm. (no. 7) and 5½mm. (no. 5) knitting needles. *The quantities of yarn given are based on average requirements and are therefore approximate.*

TENSION

14 sts. and 19 rows to 10cm. (4in.) on 5½mm. needles over pattern.

MEASUREMENTS

To fit bust: 87(91, 97)cm. (34(36, 38)in.)
Actual measurement: 117(122, 128)cm. (46(48, 50½)in.)
Length from shoulder: 68(69, 70)cm. (26¾(27, 27½)in.)
Sleeve seam: 47cm. (18½in.)
Figures in brackets refer to the larger sizes. Where only one figure is given this refers to all sizes.

ABBREVIATIONS

k. knit; *p.* purl; *st(s).* stitch(es); *inc.* increase; *dec.* decrease; *beg.* beginning; *rem.* remaining; *tog.* together; *foll.* following; *cont.* continue; *RS.* right side; *WS.* wrong side; *cm.* centimetres; *in.* inches; *mm.* millimetres; *g.* grammes; *rep.* repeat; *patt.* pattern.

BACK

With 4½mm. needles, cast on 81(85, 89) sts., and work in single rib as follows:
Row 1 (RS): K.1, * p.1, k.1, rep. from * to end.
Row 2: P.1, * k.1, p.1, rep. from * to end.
Rep. last 2 rows until rib measures 8cm. (3in.), ending with a 2nd row and working an inc. at end of last row – 82(86, 90) sts.
Change to 5½mm. needles, and work in pattern as follows:
Row 1 (RS): K.
Row 2: P.
Rep. last 2 rows 4 times more.
Row 11: K.
Row 12: K.
Rep. last 2 rows once more.
These 14 rows form the pattern and are repeated throughout.
Cont. straight in patt. until back measures 68(69, 70)cm. (26¾(27, 27½)in.) from cast-on edge, ending with a WS row.

SHAPE SHOULDERS

Keeping patt. correct, cast off 13(14, 15) sts. at beg. of next 4 rows.
Cast off rem. 30 sts.

FRONT

Work as for back until front measures 62(63, 64)cm. (24½(24¾,, 25¼)in.) from cast-on edge, ending with a WS row.

SHAPE FRONT NECK

Next row: K.33(35, 37), k.2 tog., turn, and work on this first set of sts. only.
** *Next row:* Cast off 3 sts., patt. to end.
Keeping patt. correct, dec. 1 st. at neck edge on every row until 26(28, 30) sts. remain.
Now cont. straight until front measures the same as back to beg. of shoulder shaping, ending at side edge.

SHAPE SHOULDER

Cast off 13(14, 15) sts. at beg. of next row.
Work 1 row.
Cast off rem. 13(14, 15) sts.
Return to rem. sts., rejoin yarn and cast off centre 12 sts. K.2 tog. and k. to end of row.
Work 1 row.
Now work as for first side from ** to end.

SLEEVES
(make 2)

With 4½mm. needles, cast on 37(37, 41) sts. and work in single rib as for back welt for 7cm. (2¾in.), ending with a 2nd row and working 19 incs. evenly spaced across last row – 56(56, 60) sts.
Change to 5½mm. needles, and work in patt. as for back, *at the same time*, inc. 1 st. at each end of 4th row and then every foll. 5th row until there are 84(84, 88) sts. on the needle, working inc. sts. into the patt. on either side.
Now cont. straight until sleeve measures 47cm. (18½in.) from cast-on edge, ending with a WS. row.
Cast off all sts. fairly loosely.

COLLAR

With 4½mm. needles, cast on 111 sts. and work in single rib as for back welt for 32 rows.
Cast off fairly loosely ribwise.

MAKING UP

Join both shoulder seams. With centre of cast-off edges of sleeves to shoulder seams, sew sleeves carefully in position reaching down to same depth on front and back. Join side and sleeve seams. Sew on collar, stitching the cast-on edge to neck edge, with the seam on the inside, and the two ends centred at front neck. Join collar in front, half way up, with the seam on the inside, and fold over. Press all seams.

KNIFE & FORK

FITTED SHORT-SLEEVED CASHMERE SWEATER
WITH BUTTON-DOWN NECK

MATERIALS

12(13, 14) 25 g. balls Jaeger Cashmere in cream; a pair each 2¼mm. (no. 13) and 3mm. (no. 11) knitting needles; 3 small pearl buttons; 2 safety pins.
The quantities of yarn given are based on average requirements and are therefore approximate.

TENSION

32 sts. and 40 rows to 10cm. (4in.) on 3mm. needles over st.st.

MEASUREMENTS

To fit bust: 87(91, 97)cm. (34(36, 38)in.)
Actual measurement: 96(101, 106)cm. (37¾(39¾, 41¾)in.)
Length from shoulder: 60(61, 62)cm. (23½(24, 24½)in.)
Sleeve seam: 15cm. (6in.)
Figures in brackets refer to the larger sizes. Where only one figure is given this refers to all sizes.

ABBREVIATIONS

k. knit; *p.* purl; *st(s).* stitch(es); *inc.* increase; *dec.* decrease; *st.st.* stocking stitch; *alt.* alternate; *beg.* beginning; *tog.* together; *psso.* pass slipped stitch over; *m.1* pick up horizontal loop lying between stitch just worked and following stitch and work into the back of it; *rem.* remaining; *cont.* continue; *rep.* repeat; *cm.* centimetres; *mm.* millimetres; *in.* inches; *g.* grammes; *RS.* right side; *WS.* wrong side; *sl.* slip; *foll.* following.

BACK

With 2¼mm. needles, cast on 153(161, 169) sts. by the thumb method, and work in single rib as follows:

Row 1: K.1, * p.1, k.1, rep. from * to end.
Row 2: P.1, * k.1, p.1, rep. from * to end.
Rep. last 2 rows until 23 rows in all have been worked.
Change to 3mm. needles and starting with a k. row work in st.st. for 20 rows.

WORK SHAPINGS

Next row (RS): K.38(40, 42), sl. 1, k.2 tog., psso. (called dec. 2), k.71(75, 79), dec. 2, k.38(40, 42).
Starting with a p. row work in st.st. for 3 rows.
Next row: K.37(39, 41), dec. 2, k.69(73, 77), dec. 2, k.37(39, 41).
Starting with a p. row work in st.st. for 3 rows.
Cont. in this way and dec. on next row and then every foll. 4th row as set, working 1 st. less at beg. and end of each dec. row and 2 sts. less at centre until 117(125, 133) sts. remain, ending with a dec. row.
Starting with a p. row work in st.st. for 19 rows.
* *Next row (RS):* K.30(32, 34), m.1, k. to last 30(32, 34) sts., m.1, k. to end.
Starting with a p. row work in st.st. for 3 rows.
Rep. from * until there are 153(161, 169) sts. on the needle, ending with 1 row worked in st.st. after inc. row, thus ending with a WS row.**

SHAPE ARMHOLES

Cast off 8 sts. at beg. of next 2 rows. Now dec. 1 st. at each end of every foll. alt. row until 113(121, 129) sts. remain.
Now cont. straight until back measures 20(21, 22)cm. (8(8¼, 8¾)in.) from beg. of armhole shaping, ending with a RS row.

SHAPE SHOULDERS AND BACK NECK

Next row: P.37(41, 45), cast off centre 39 sts., p. to end of row and work on this last set of sts. only.
Cast off 11(12, 13) sts. at beg. of next row and foll. alt. row, *at the same time*, dec. 1 st. at neck edge on next 4 rows.
Cast off rem. 11(13, 15) sts.
With RS facing rejoin yarn to rem. sts., and dec. 1 st. at neck edge on next 4 rows, *at the same time*, cast off 11(12, 13) sts. at

beg. of foll. 2 alt. rows.
Cast off rem. 11(13, 15) sts.

FRONT

Work as for back to **.

SHAPE ARMHOLES AND FRONT NECK OPENING

Next row (RS): Cast off 8 sts., k.64(68, 72), slip the next 9 sts. onto a safety pin, turn, and work on this first set of sts. only.
Dec. 1 st. at armhole edge on every foll. alt. row until 52(56, 60) sts. remain.
Now work straight until front measures 12(13, 14) cm. (4¾(5, 5½)in.) from beg. of armhole shaping, ending at centre front edge.

SHAPE NECK

Cast off 6 sts. at beg. (neck edge) of next row and 5 sts. at beg. of foll. alt. row.
Now dec. 1 st. at same edge on every row until 33(37, 41) sts. remain.
Now work straight until front measures the same as back to beg. of shoulder shaping, ending at armhole edge.

SHAPE SHOULDER

Cast off 11(12, 13) sts. at beg. of next row and foll. alt. row. Work 1 row.
Cast off rem. 11(13, 15) sts.
With RS facing rejoin yarn to rem. sts., and work to match first side, reversing all shapings.

SLEEVES
(make 2)

With 2¼mm. needles, cast on 97(105, 113) sts. by the thumb method, and work in single rib as for back welt for 7 rows, and work 8 incs. evenly spaced across last row – 105(113, 121) sts.
Change to 3mm. needles, and starting with a k. row work in st.st. for 52 rows.

SHAPE TOP

Cast off 8 sts. at beg. of next 2 rows.
Now dec. 1 st. at each end of every foll. alt. row until 65(73, 81) sts. remain.
Work 9 rows straight.
Now dec. 1 st. at each end of every row until 29 sts. remain.
Next row: Cast off, working k.1, (k.2 tog.) to end.
Join both shoulder seams.

FRONT BANDS

With 2¼mm. needles, and working over the 9 sts. at front neck opening, work in k.1, p.1, rib for 10 rows, working 3 incs. evenly spaced along 1st row – 12 sts.
Buttonhole row (RS): Rib 5, cast off 2 sts., rib to end.
Next row: Rib 5, cast on 2 sts., rib to end.
Rib 16 more rows.
Rep. the 2 buttonhole rows again, then rib a further 12 rows, sewing band in position as you go along.
Leave sts. on a safety pin.
With 2¼mm. needles, cast on 12 sts. and work another band to match, but omit buttonholes.
Leave sts. on a safety pin.

NECKBAND

With 2¼mm. needles and RS facing, rib over the 12 sts. of buttonhole band, then pick up and k. 40 sts. up right front neck, 50 sts. along back neck, 40 sts. down left front neck and finally rib over the 12 sts. of button band – 154 sts.
Now work in single rib as set for the front bands. Work 3 rows. Rep. the 2 buttonhole rows again, then rib a further 4 rows.
Cast off fairly loosely ribwise.

MAKING UP

With centre of sleeve tops to shoulder seams, sew sleeves carefully into armholes gathering top slightly to fit. Join side and sleeve seams. Stitch button band behind buttonhole band at base. Sew on buttons to correspond with buttonholes.

USEFUL ADDRESSES

FOR ADVICE ABOUT YARN:

Pingouin (French Wools Ltd.)
7–11 Lexington Street,
London W1R 4BU
Tel: 01–439 8891

*Patons and Baldwin Ltd.,
and Jaeger Handknitting*
Alloa, Clackmannanshire,
Scotland FK10 1EG
Tel: 0259 723431

Filatura di Crosa (Mail order service)
7 Knights Arcade,
Knightsbridge, London SW1
Tel: 01–584 9533

Rowan Yarns
Green Lane Mill,
Holmfirth, W. Yorks.
Tel: 0484 686714

Emu Wools Ltd
Leeds Road, Greengates,
Bradford, W. Yorks. BD10 9TE
Tel: 0274 614031

Sirdar PLC
Flanshaw Lane,
Alverthorpe,
Wakefield, W. Yorks. WF2 9ND
Tel: 0924 371501

Phildar
4 Gambrel Road,
Westgate Industrial Estate,
Northampton NN5 5NF
Tel: 0604 583111/6

Avocet
Hammerain House,
Hookstone Avenue,
Harrogate, N. Yorks. HG2 8ER
Tel: 0423 871440

Scheepjeswol (UK) Ltd.
PO Box 48,
7 Colemeadow Road,
Redditch, Worcs. B98 9NZ
Tel: 0527 61056

WOOL SHOPS TO VISIT:

Colourspun
18A Camden Road,
London NW1 9HA
Tel: 01-267 6317

Creativity
37 New Oxford Street, London W1
Tel: 01-240 2945

Ries Wools
242–243 High Holborn,
London WC1V 7DZ
Tel: 01-242 7721

OVERSEAS ADDRESSES

PATONS & JAEGER

USA
C. J. Bates and Sons Ltd.,
Route 9a,
Chester,
Connecticut 06412

Canada agent
Patons & Baldwins (Canada) Ltd.,
1001 Roselawn Avenue,
Toronto, Ontario M6B 1B8

Australia agent
Coats & Patons Aust. Ltd.,
321–355 Fern Tree Gully Road,
P.O. Box 110,
Mount Waverley, Victoria 3149

S. Africa
Marketing Manager,
Patons & Baldwins (S. Africa) Pty. Ltd.,
P.O. Box 33, Randfontein 1760

PINGOUIN

Head office and mail order
BP 9110, 59061 Roubaix,
Cedex 1, France

USA agent
Pingouin-Promafil Corp. (USA),
P.O. Box 100, Highway 45,
Jamestown, S. Carolina 29453

Canada agent
Promafil (Canada) Ltd,
1500 Rue Jules Poitras,
379 St Laurent,
Quebec H4N 1X7

Australia stockist
The Needlewoman,
308 Centrepoint,
Murray Street,
Hobart, Tasmania 7000

S. Africa agent
Romatex/Yarns and Wools
P.O. Box 12, Jacobs 4026,
Natal

ROWAN

USA
Westminster Trading,
5 Northern Blvd, Amhurst,
New Hampshire 03031

Canada
Estelle,
38 Continental Place,
Scarborough,
Ontario M1R 2TH

Australia
Sunspun,
195 Canterbury Road,
Canterbury 3126

New Zealand
Creative Fashion Centre,
P.O. Box 45083,
Epuni Railway, Lower Hutt

South Africa
Jumpers, Shop 17,
Admiral's Court,
31 Tyrwhitt Avenue,
Rosebank 2196, Johannesburg

SIRDAR

USA distributor
Kendex Corp., P.O. Box 1909,
Moorpark, California 93020

Canada distributors
Diamond Yarn (Canada) Corp.,
153 Bridgeland Ave,
Unit 11, Toronto,
Ontario M6A 2Y6

Diamond Yarn (Canada) Corp.,
9697 St. Lawrence Blvd.,
Montreal, Quebec H3L 2N1

Australia distributor
Sirdar (Australia) Pty Ltd.,
P.O. Box 110,
Mount Waverley, Victoria 3149

New Zealand distributor
Alltex International,
106 Parnell Road,
P.O. Box 2500, Auckland

South Africa distributor
Patons and Baldwins,
P.O. Box 33, Randfontein 1760

FOR EMBROIDERY EQUIPMENT:

John Lewis
Oxford Street, London W1
Tel: 01-629 7711

Dickins and Jones
Regent Street, London W1
Tel: 01-734 7070
George Street,
Richmond, Surrey
Tel: 01-940 7761

Liberty
Regent Street, London W1
Tel: 01-734 1234

FOR BUTTONS:

The Button Box
44 Bedford Street,
London WC2E 9HA
Tel: 01-240 2841

BEADS AND SEQUINS:

Ells and Farrier Ltd (Mail order service)
The Bead House,
20 Princes Street (off Hanover Sq),
London W1R 8PH
Tel: 01-629 9964

EMBROIDERY THREADS:

DMC
Dunlicraft,
Pullman Rd,
Leicester
Tel: 0533 811040

KNITTING KITS

All the designs in the embroidery section, as well as many other designs in this book, are available as knitting kits.
For further details write to:
Angela Knit Kits
14 Batley Field Hill,
Batley,
W. Yorks. WF17 5SD
Tel: 0924 476437

DEP. LEGAL B-32.822-88